D0984616

The Working Parent's Survival Guide

The Working Parent's Survival Guide

How to Parent Smarter Not Harder

Anita Cleare

ROWMAN & LITTLEFIELD
Lanham • Boulder • New York • London

Published by Rowman & Littlefield
An imprint of The Rowman & Littlefield Publishing Group, Inc.
4501 Forbes Boulevard, Suite 200, Lanham, Maryland 20706
www.rowman.com

6 Tinworth Street, London SE11 5AL, United Kingdom

British Library Cataloguing in Publication Information Available

Library of Congress Cataloging-in-Publication Data

Names: Cleare, Anita, 1968- author.
Title: The working parent's survival guide : how to parent smarter not harder/ Anita Cleare.
Description: Lanham, Maryland : Rowman & Littlefield, [2021] | Includes bibliographical references and index. | Summary: "The Working Parent's Guide to Positive Parenting shows you how to be a great parent by parenting smarter not harder and by understanding what children really need from us. Offering strategies for focusing on what really matters, connecting with our kids, and meeting everyone's needs, Anita Cleare guides working parents to building a happier family"—Provided by publisher.
Identifiers: LCCN 2020054903 (print) | LCCN 2020054904 (ebook) | ISBN 9781538152430 (cloth ; alk. paper) | ISBN 9781538152447 (electronic)
Subjects: LCSH: Parenting. | Parent and child. | Families.
Classification: LCC HQ755.8 .C567 2021 (print) | LCC HQ755.8 (ebook) | DDC 649/.1—dc23
LC record available at https://lccn.loc.gov/2020054903
LC ebook record available at https://lccn.loc.gov/2020054904

Contents

Part Three: Balancing Well-Being and Workload

Acknowledgments

I have been deeply inspired and moved by the many parents I have worked with over the years—their stories and struggles are written on every page of this book. Our children are so precious to us, and when things seem to be going awry, the hurt and anxiety can be hard to bear. I feel privileged that so many parents have let me into their lives and entrusted me with their truest thoughts and feelings. It is through these real lives that I have learned what makes a difference.

Many of the tips in this book have been picked up from other parents or from fellow professionals and family support colleagues, as well as from my Triple P® training. I have loved being continually surprised by the things children get up to and by the brilliant responses (and wondrous contortions!) of their parents.

I am grateful to all the followers of my blog *Thinking Parenting* who have urged and encouraged me through the writing of this book. I can't tell you what a difference it has made knowing that you were looking forward to reading it! My thanks also go to my agent, Anna Power, for believing in me, and to my husband, Ivan Palmer, who deserves the highest accolades for supporting me 100 percent no matter what.

And of course I have to acknowledge my own children who, in addition to being the most amazing kids ever (and a continual source of pride and wonder), have also helped me personally to experience most of the challenges known in modern parenthood. Being your mom has stretched me beyond what I thought I was capable of, in every direction, and loving you has been the making of me.

Introduction

Toward a Family Life That Is Good for You and Your Children

Most working parents feel like we are running just to stand still. We want to be good parents. We want to get parenting "right." But we have limited time, limited energy, limited patience, and too much to do. And we are seldom at our best at the end of a working day when the parenting shift kicks in.

Modern family life has undergone a seismic shift in the past two decades. The majority of parents in the United Kingdom now work. We work longer hours and commute farther to work, and we are frequently stretched to the limits. A typical working parent's day is tightly timed between drop-offs and pick-ups. And with little slack for unforeseeables, this finely balanced juggling act is quickly derailed when our child refuses to cooperate or their big emotions bubble over. At the end of the day, we rush home to herd our children through a relentless timetable of clubs, homework, dinner, and bath, while all the time feeling guilty because we know they just want our attention (but we just want them to stick to the schedule and go to bed).

Modern parents are working more and parenting more, and with only a limited number of hours available, something's got to give. For many working parents, it's our own well-being that's being jettisoned. Huge swathes of family time now revolve around activities aimed at children (petting farms, theme parks, birthday parties, children's sports) rather than relaxation time for adults. Every Sunday as a child, I was carted to a cricket ground and left to my own devices on a random slide, swing, or patch of grass while my dad captained the second eleven. Now adults are much more likely to spend their weekends tagging along to children's sports.

1

Yet working parents are guilt-ridden about lack of time with our children. We pack extra parenting into every opportunity. We buy toys and gadgets that claim to boost children's development. We spend our nonworking hours ferrying children to musical, sporting, and educational activities to give them the best start in life. We want the world for our kids, so we try to carve out the straightest route to happiness for them. We beaver away, removing obstacles from their paths to save them from discomforts and difficult experiences. We wish for them always to fit in and do well and never to be left out or be sad or upset. We work even longer hours or even farther away so we can live in a better house or send them to a better school or just afford all those clubs and sports we take them to in our "free" time. Anxious that we are not doing enough, we try to do more and more.

But we still worry it isn't enough. At best, working parents feel like we are keeping our heads above water. At worst, many of us just feel like we're failing. Our children are certainly not grateful, despite our gargantuan efforts. Because, ironically, although parents are prioritizing children more, we are understanding them less. Children are getting fewer of those things that really do help their development, like outdoor free play, risk-taking, conversational turns, and consistent boundaries. With too much guilt and no energy, we don't have the patience to tune in to how our children are thinking and feeling or work out how to motivate them or positively manage their difficult behavior. We are so shattered from trying to do it all that it's almost impossible to stick to our guns and make good parenting decisions. Or, if we do stand firm, we feel like the perpetual Bad Guy. There are just so many decisions to make, and all of them feel crucial.

This book is about moving the goalposts. It's about doing less, not more. It's about parenting in a way that is good for your children but also good for you, which builds your happiness and nurtures your well-being rather than stretching you so thin that you are in danger of breaking. It's about parenting smarter by understanding how your children think and what they really need from you.

Maybe you are a mom heading back to work who wants advice on how to squeeze being a parent into fewer hours. Or perhaps you're a dad who's fallen into a stressed-out parenting hole and wants to stop shouting your kids out of the house in the mornings. Maybe you only have a few hours a week with your children and you're struggling to connect. Or you are just tired of going around in circles trying to fit more work and more parenting into a finite number of hours. This is the book for you.

The Working Parent's Survival Guide brings together three essential elements for being a happy working parent:

1. A clear picture of what children really need, what makes them tick, and what drives children's development, drawn from developmental psychology.
2. Practical tools and hands-on parenting solutions from my real-world work supporting families.
3. An actionable blueprint for how you can enhance your personal well-being based on the happiness-building ideas of positive psychology.

This book collects in one place all the proven, practical strategies that I have witnessed make such a difference to the lives of the parents I work with. Its big ambition is to help you build a happy family life, but the focus is on small doable changes and how you can use those little bits of time when work is done to create a positive family environment, an environment you all want to be a part of. My goal is to empower all working parents to have a family life that is low on conflict, high in warmth, and good for children's development. But also good for you. A family that balances adults' and children's needs, in which kids can thrive and parents flourish.

Positive psychology is all about understanding what makes life feel worthwhile so that we can do more of it. It focuses on positive experiences, states, and traits and asks how we can create more of these in our lives in order to optimize our well-being. Sounds simple, doesn't it?! But positive psychology becomes a bit trickier when it comes to parenting. Because parenting is not just about the feel-good factor. Parents have a responsibility to teach children the skills they need to be successful adults. And that inevitably involves setting boundaries and responding when children get things wrong.

Managing children's behavior when you are tired and stressed is doubly difficult. When our energy reserves are low and our stress levels are high, it's easy to slip into negative habits, like constantly battling with your children, resorting to shouting or just giving in. Effective discipline strategies are a game changer for working parents. My aim is not only to give you the practical tools to parent positively but also to help you step inside your child's mind and understand what drives their behavior. Because when we understand where our children are coming from, it makes it much easier to connect with their way of thinking and respond to their behavior in a thoughtful and intentioned way.

Bringing together positive parenting and positive psychology involves identifying and building on our children's strengths. It means understanding which of our own habits and characteristics are most effective for supporting our child's development and finding ways to switch off from work mode in order to deploy our more playful, empathetic parent mode more often. It means looking for the real enjoyment in family life, for the win–wins that meet our children's developmental needs but that also increase our own well-being. And that means learning to manage our own triggers and hotspots so that we are able to rise to the challenge of being a parent.

This book is not a contribution to the stay-at-home versus working parent debate. I won't help you solve the question "To work or not to work?" or tell you the ideal working pattern to guarantee family well-being. Because it is not the exact number of hours you do or don't work that makes the difference. It's how you manage your own stress and how you create meaningful connections with your children in whatever time you have available that really matters.

The Working Parent's Survival Guide outlines an approach to parenting that aims to balance the needs of the whole family but that can be realistically fit into modern working patterns. It covers key challenges, such as how to manage bickering siblings when you are tired at the end of the day, and common concerns, such as controlling children's tech time and promoting good self-esteem. Plus, there's a focus on those sticky parts of a working parent's day like getting kids out of the house in the morning and avoiding Sunday night homework battles. The focus is on practical ideas and real-world wins to build family happiness and support both children's and parents' well-being—everyday actions to help you create the family life you want to come home to.

If you are a time-poor parent who wants to be a good parent, this book is for you. Whether you are a mom or a dad, work full time or part time, or see your children for only a few hours a week or you are taking the full brunt of parenting solo on top of working, this book will help you make the most of your time with your children. It's aimed primarily at parents with children under twelve years old (managing teenagers' challenging behavior requires slightly different approaches!), but the principle of doing less but connecting more applies to all ages. To be inclusive, I switch from assuming you have daughters, sons, one child, or several—all are welcome!

This book is a chance for you to get off the treadmill for a moment and reach a deeper understanding of what your child needs from you and what you want from your family. It might lead you to completely reset your family life. Or it might just help you to tweak your parenting approach. But when you are in the thick of it, it's easy to miss those small changes that could make a big difference. So sit back, grab a cup of tea, and let's start by thinking about what's really going on in your family.

I

MEANINGFUL MOMENTS

1

Time-Poor Parenting Traps

There's no such thing as a perfect parent. Parenting is not something that anyone gets completely right. We learn how to do it through experience, and that means sometimes getting it wrong (just hopefully not too wrong). The best any of us can aim for is to learn from our mistakes quickly and try not to repeat them too often. Good parenting is about reflecting on what you are doing, noticing what works, catching yourself doing unhelpful things, and trying to do them a little less often. There is nothing anyone can give you—no psychological trick, no magic wand or witch's spell—that you can use to control your children's behavior or guarantee their happiness. The only thing that any of us can control is ourselves. Parenting isn't really about managing children's behavior; it's about managing our own thoughts, feelings, and actions. So let's start with a bit of a self-audit.

PARENTING HOLES

The purpose of this audit is not to make you feel bad, so please don't use it as a stick to beat yourself with. But there are some common pitfalls and bad habits that working parents can fall into. I call these "parenting holes." Some of us fall into all of these parenting holes at one time or another. And some of us have a few favorite holes that we get stuck in again and again. But we all fall into a parenting hole at some point.

Working parents are especially vulnerable to parenting holes that involve guilt or anxiety about not having enough time with our children. When we feel like time is short, it's easy to opt for short-term quick-fix solutions and fall into parenting habits that are helpful in the immediate moment but that create problems in the longer term. The parenting holes that working parents are especially prone to include

- wanting all family time to be lovely,
- giving in to avoid conflict,
- inconsistency,
- focusing on children's problem behavior,
- negative thinking, and
- parenting on autopilot.

As parents we all find ourselves in a hole from time to time. The trick is to recognize these traps as quickly as possible and try not to fall into them too often. So let's start by asking, "Which hole am I in?"

"Good parenting is not about getting it all right all of the time."

Wanting It All to Be Lovely

When we have limited time with our children, it creates huge pressure for that time to be special, enjoyable, and conflict-free. No parent wants to come home after a long day at work (or a whole week of waiting to see them) and battle with our children. We long for those sepia-tinted family times that happy memories are made of, those treasured days filled with ice cream, sunshine, and laughter that we look back on so fondly from our own childhoods.

The problem is, expecting all family time to be lovely is simply unrealistic. Those cherished childhood memories are actually edited versions of reality that leave out the bits where big brother shouted, dad sulked, and mom cried. No parent ever spent an entire day with a small child without somebody crying (and not always the child!). So if undiluted special time is what we expect, we are going to be disappointed—in ourselves and in our children. When we set the bar that high, family time is always going to feel like a failure.

Parenting hole number one goes like this: "Family time has been scheduled for Sunday afternoon, after football practice and before homework. Everyone will be jolly, kind to each other, and there will be no tears or tantrums."

Only it doesn't work that way, does it? The kids bicker, your eldest son refuses to join in, your youngest cries when she loses at Buckaroo, and your partner finds an urgent chore to escape to. And then you go looking for someone to blame—yourself, your partner, your children. . . . Because 100 percent lovely usually turns out to be "a bit of a nightmare with a few OK moments."

Wanting all family time to be special time not only leads to disappointment, it often leads to self-blame ("I must be a terrible parent if I can't even have a nice day with my kids") or to negative thinking about our children ("My kids are so ungrateful they can't even behave themselves when I do something nice for them"). It also frequently leads to conflict between parents. While one parent aims to dish out nothing but ice cream, the other parent gets sucked into the reality vacuum of drawing boundaries and disciplining (the classic good cop/bad cop parenting trap). In our desperation to avoid tears or tantrums, this doomed pursuit of perfect family time ultimately leads to contorting ourselves out of shape or relaxing all limits just to keep the children happy. Which brings us to parenting hole number two: giving in to avoid conflict.

Giving in to Avoid Conflict

Putting boundaries in place and enforcing limits are key to effective parenting. They oil the wheels of family life, keep kids safe and healthy, and teach them the skills they need for life. But enforcing boundaries inevitably involves conflict. Children don't like parents' boundaries. Why would they? Those boundaries are usually there to stop them doing things they want to do (like eating ice cream for breakfast, lunch, and dinner). So kids push back against boundaries. Again and again and again. If you are looking to reduce conflict in your family life, relaxing boundaries and giving in to children's pushback seems like a logical quick-fix solution for keeping the peace.

This parenting hole goes like this: "I desperately want what little time I have with my children to be special and enjoyable and I am way too tired for a battle about eating vegetables/polite behavior/whining/bedtime* [*delete as appropriate]. It's much easier to give them what they want. I know it might come back to bite me tomorrow, but at least I'll have a pleasant day today."

And in the short term, it could work. If you are on holiday, great! Holidays are all about breaking out of routine, staying up late, and eating too much ice cream. Maybe if you are on a day trip, too, some rules might be relaxed. But holidays and day trips can be presented as exceptions. If you are giving in to avoid conflict just because you've had a hard day at work, your child is going to find it impossible to understand when the rules apply and when they don't.

Avoiding conflict might work in the immediate moment, but it has the opposite effect in the longer term. Because by pushing back at boundaries, children test whether those limits are absolute or negotiable. Every time a particular boundary is broken, it teaches your child that this limit can definitely be got around if they use the right strategy. And children repeat behavior that gets positive results. By giving in or reversing our decisions when children push back at the rules, we accidentally reward that pushback behavior and therefore make it more likely to happen again. If the pushback is successful, children will do it again and again. There will be more conflict in the long run, not less. And home becomes the battleground we were desperately trying to avoid.

"Giving in to avoid conflict makes it more likely that parents will end up shouting."

By giving in to keep the peace, we often push ourselves to our limits and end up parenting rashly or inappropriately. Picture this: your kids are playing a jumping game on the sofa. You tell them to stop in case someone gets hurt, but they ignore you. They are having a great time! You tell them again to stop but are answered with happy squeals of laughter. So you leave them to it. You let it go. They are enjoying themselves so much it would be a shame to spoil it. The laughter gets louder and the play gets more boisterous. Those happy squeals are really loud now and the cushions are all over the floor. A drink gets spilled. And one of them has knocked over the lamp and banged his head. You reach your patience limit and "Bang!" Suddenly you are shouting and the kids are crying.

Giving in to avoid conflict results in greater conflict in the long run.

Sometimes it's guilt that fuels this particular parenting hole. Working parents who feel guilty about spending time apart from their children are far more likely to give in to whining or complaining. It's hard to stick to your principles and impose appropriate boundaries when your child is screaming "You're mean!" and a little voice inside your head is telling you "She's right, it's all my fault." When we feel guilty about not spending enough time with our children, it's easy to forget that children misbehave *because they are children*. Not because you go to work.

This particular parenting hole is not unrelated to habit number three: inconsistency.

Inconsistency

I can't imagine there is a parent out there who hasn't heard that consistency in parenting is important. But why, and how can we achieve it? Because let's face it, consistent parenting is easier on some days than others. When you are well rested, unstressed, and have had a good day, sticking to your plan in the face of a protesting child is achievable. But what are the chances of you being well rested and unstressed as a working parent with a young child?

"Give me a good night's sleep, a successful commute, an easy day at work, and I'm a great parent! I set rules, I follow through and 'No' always means 'No.' When the kids start bickering, I sort it out calmly, firmly, and fairly. But on a tough day? When the jibes start to fly, you'll find me hiding in the cupboard under the stairs with my hands over my ears hoping they sort it out without anyone losing a limb." Sound familiar?

Now I'm not comparing your children to mice or birds, but let's take a detour via "Skinner's Box." Skinner was a psychologist in the 1930s who explored the effects of consistency on the speed at which animals learn. He designed a box with a lever that animals could press in order to release a pellet of food. What he found was that when the pellet of food was delivered consistently every single time the animal pressed the lever, those animals learned very quickly to repeat that behavior when they were hungry. When a pellet of food was released only sometimes (that is, inconsistently), those animals learned the link between lever pressing and food delivery much more slowly. And when a pellet of food was never released, those animals quickly stopped bothering to press the lever at all. Consistency promotes quicker learning.

Interestingly, those animals that received food pellets inconsistently were seen pressing the lever repeatedly even when they weren't hungry, stockpiling food that they didn't need because they were never sure when it would/wouldn't be there. And they were very slow to adapt to change. Even when the lever stopped producing food at all, they would keep pressing it. Inconsistent responses promote inconsistent behavior.

Now imagine a child in a supermarket who wants a doughnut. If making a big, noisy fuss never results in them getting a doughnut, that child will quickly abandon their making a fuss strategy. Or if they are consistently rewarded for staying quietly in their trolley with a doughnut at the end of the shopping trip, they will quickly learn to stay quietly in the trolley every time. But if making a big, noisy fuss sometimes (that is, inconsistently) gets the doughnut, they will keep trying and make more fuss more often. Even if they don't really want a doughnut. Inconsistency in parenting increases children's difficult behavior.

If you are not sure whether you have fallen into the inconsistency parenting hole, here's a quick litmus test. Is your child one of those kids who is well behaved at school but a real challenge at home? When you describe your child's behavior to their teacher, do they look at you in disbelief? Like they have no recognition of the child you are describing? Well, that could be a sign that your child is thriving on the clear rules and consistent responses they get at school but is unsettled by inconsistent or overly flexible boundaries at home.

I Am the Behavior Police

Being consistent, however, does not mean constantly picking our children up on every single thing they do wrong. When you only have an hour to parent, it's tempting to zoom in on children's bad behavior and try to cram as much instruction and correction as possible into the limited time available. Working parents are especially prone to this particular trap because we have to be so exceptionally organized to get everything done.

This parenting hole goes like this: "I haven't got much time, I need to do all my parenting in the next hour. What have you done today that I need to correct you on? No, you can't do/say/eat/watch/read* that [*delete as appropriate]. To make up for lost parenting time, I am going to reinforce every single boundary all in one go and prove to all and sundry (aka myself) that I am totally on the case when it comes to parenting."

For a child, that's not a lot of fun to be on the end of. And it doesn't really work. Because nine times out of ten, it involves paying far more attention to the behavior we want them to stop than to the behavior we want to encourage, which is a problem because children tend to repeat behavior that gets attention.

Imagine this. The kids are playing quietly (for once). They're not fighting over the remote control or bickering about whose turn it is or yelling for help, string, cookies, or anything else. So what do you do? You make the most of a precious moment to sit down and have a cup of tea. (Or, more likely, you run around trying to complete the million jobs you have to do as part of your second shift.) As long as the kids are doing nothing wrong, they are well and truly ignored. Until the screaming starts, that is. Then we go thundering in at full throttle in behavior police mode to sort out their misdemeanors.

What do children learn from this? They learn that bad behavior is what gets mom or dad's attention. They learn that there is nothing more guaranteed to get attention than hitting their younger sister over the head with a heavy object. Playing nicely with her gets no attention, so why bother? When we ignore kids when they get it right and pay lots of attention when they get it wrong, we inadvertently encourage them to keep up the bad behavior.

Paying too much attention to children's misbehavior is also often linked to bad habit number five: negative thinking.

Negative Thinking

This particular parenting hole usually takes the form of putting the blame squarely on our children's shoulders for their difficult behavior. When a child is demonstrating challenging behavior, it's easy to label them negatively: "He's so mean," "She's so stubborn," "She does that just to annoy me." These are negative thinking habits.

When parents call me up for support, they don't usually say, "I'm having problems with my parenting." What they say is, "I'm having problems with my child." But if we place the blame on our child for their behavior, we can get stuck in a negative spiral: "My child needs to change. It's her fault we are arguing." That type of blame thinking often means we miss our own role in the dynamic. We don't see how we contribute to our child's behavior patterns. Therefore we don't notice how we could make small changes to our own behavior to get a different result from our child.

When it works well, parenting can feel very simple: "I do X, my child does Y, the result is positive and we both learn to do the same things again." Yay—a virtuous circle. In general, though, things are less straightforward. Often our first attempts don't work well ("I do X, my child does not do Y") and we have to adapt and adjust our parenting accordingly. We learn, for example, that this particular child does not cope well with surprises or is uncooperative on an empty stomach. And we adapt. Maybe we learn to do Z instead of X if we want to get Y.

But sometimes adapting can be hard and we keep doing the same thing because we think it ought to be working. We get stuck in a negative rut. Then every time I do X and my child does not do Y it feels very hurtful, a criticism of me as a parent and what I hold dear. We experience our child's behavior as a judgment on us as parents or as a result of something "wrong" with the child that needs to be fixed.

And so we don't adapt, we dig in. We label our child negatively and the parenting hole gets bigger. And we feel less and less competent as parents and begin to label ourselves negatively too. Their behavior gets worse and our relationship with our child starts to deteriorate. We get well and truly stuck in that negative thinking hole.

Parenting on Autopilot

This final parenting hole is particularly easy to fall into when you are tired, worried, or just withdrawing because it all feels too much. You are physically there, with your child, but your mind is well and truly on other things. You are present but absent.

Maybe you are in the house but too busy with other things to interact with your child. Maybe you are at the park, even pushing your child on a swing, but your head is in your phone and you are not really listening to anything your child is saying. Or maybe you are just firmly locked inside your own head and thoughts. You are physically present, but you are not in any meaningful way available to your children. You are parenting on autopilot.

I am particularly prone to this behavior in times of stress. I have been known—genuinely—not to hear people when they talk to me. Nothing gets through the firewall. I may nod when spoken to but will have no recollection whatsoever of having been told anything because my brain was too busy processing all the other things it needed to think about.

Being a working parent can be ridiculously hectic. When you get home is when the hard work starts. Children need to be fed and washed and read to. There are spellings to learn, clubs to attend, dinner to cook, a house to tidy, grass to mow, food to buy, clothes to wash—the list is endless. And when your child wants a piece of you, it's easy to say, "Not now, I'm busy," or just nod half-heartedly.

But what are we signaling when we do that? Our children quickly learn that we are unavailable to them emotionally. That they need to escalate their behavior to a fever pitch in order to be noticed. That cooking dinner is more important than listening to them. That connecting with them is not valued. And it's not just children who miss out when parents are on autopilot; parents lose too. We miss all our children's subtle cues, those little signals that help us understand them, how they think and what they are feeling. We miss out on the richness of that relationship and reduce ourselves to a task-focused childminder role.

Parenting on autopilot means our children are safe and supervised and their physical needs are met. But not much more. If you aspire to a richer family life, it's a parenting hole you don't want to spend too much time in. Finding a way to switch off from tasks, plans, and preoccupations and connect with your child is essential for building a happy family life.

THINKING POINT

Look back through the parenting holes. Which one(s) do you regularly fall into? Are there particular situations or times of the day when you are most likely to resort to unrealistic expectations, unhelpful strategies, or negative thinking?

So there you have it: six parenting holes for time-poor parents. Were any of those familiar? Which hole are you in? Maybe a bit of all of them? That's OK. Understanding what we are currently doing is the first step to making positive changes. What matters is not that you fell into a hole but that you recognize it and take steps to get out of it. Parenting is a habit, and habits can be changed—doing things even just a little bit differently can have surprisingly big results. The first step is to get yourself into the right mindset. Cue chapter 2!

2

Work-Me versus Parent-Me

The biggest challenge for most working parents is simply arriving home after a day at work in the right frame of mind to parent. It sounds simple enough but, for many of us, that involves learning how to be two different people on the same day.

Modern workplaces require adults to be task focused and efficiency driven. Our working days revolve around targets and deadlines. Employers want work completed on time and within budget. Doing well at work means sticking to schedules, getting through tasks as efficiently as possible, focusing on measurable outcomes, and always keeping up the pace. It's hardly surprising so many of us find work stressful—it takes a lot of resources to sustain that level of hyperefficiency, even when we are enjoying it.

But when it comes to family life, our workplace skill set is not necessarily a good fit. Children need us to deploy different strengths. They need emotionally attuned parents who are curious, playful, and empathetic; who can slow down and pick up on their subtle cues; and who aren't fixated on immediate end goals. They need parents who can prioritize reflecting and listening over getting the job done and who can support their learning not by pushing them to hit a target but by making the learning process meaningful.

Being a calm, consistent parent after a long day at work is not easy. Good parenting means standing your ground when children push back at boundaries. It means tuning in to your child and managing your own emotions in the face of a child who has not yet mastered theirs. That's a big ask at the end of a long working day. The skills you deploy at work are unlikely to be the same as the skills you'll need for the parenting shift. Learning to switch between work mode and parent mode is essential for creating a family life that meets everyone's needs.

UNDERSTANDING YOUR WORK MODE

For most working parents, our work lives involve a big helping of what I call "efficiency thinking." This is a type of future-minded thinking that focuses on getting the job done with minimum waste of time or effort. It prioritizes the completion of a series of tasks in a way that achieves an end goal effectively and in the most efficient way possible.

Now, obviously, all jobs are a bit different. Where you sit within the production chain will influence how much efficiency thinking you use (as will your underlying temperament). But there are very few jobs in the modern world that don't require employees to work to some sort of schedule or quota. Even those of us working in people-focused caring professions have to keep one eye at all times on targets and budgets. In the workplace, time is money (and money is king).

Most of us want to get on in the workplace because we care about what we do, because we want to progress up the ladder, or simply because we want to keep our paychecks coming in. Being good at our jobs is important. Perhaps our job defines who we are and how we feel about ourselves. Or maybe we feel responsible (for clients, for colleagues, for putting bread on the table). But it can feel like there is a lot at stake. Work matters. So we get good at this task-focused efficiency thinking. We quickly learn to prioritize efficiency in order to thrive (or just survive) in the workplace. We spend our days in hyper-efficient mode, constantly running through to-do lists, vigilantly seeking out problems, solutions, and threats to our position. We practice efficiency thinking again and again and again until we get really good at it and it becomes second nature.

Then when we get home, it can be really hard to switch it off again. Which is difficult. Because children don't do efficiency thinking.

Why Children Don't Do Efficiency Thinking

Children don't do efficiency thinking because they can't. They have other developmental priorities and their brains just aren't wired that way. The part of the brain that enables us to think efficiently is called the prefrontal cortex. It sits at the front of the brain just behind the forehead. The prefrontal cortex governs complex executive functions such as strategic thinking, planning, and evaluating. It is this part of the brain that enables us to focus on a goal, plan a sequence of tasks, and resist distractions. In adults, the prefrontal cortex is fully developed (which is just as well because it is so valuable in our working lives). But in children it is still a work in progress. Although children look like completed humans from the outside (just a little smaller), young children's brains are really only half-finished. A child's brain is not a small-sized version of an adult brain. It's more like an earlier software edition that lacks key functionality and processing power.

The part of the adult brain that engages in efficiency thinking is not yet fully operational in a young child. Parents' task-focused, distraction-inhibiting, goal-oriented work mode is completely alien to a child. For you, the purpose of a particular walk might be to get to the shops, buy milk, and get home as quickly as possible so you can put dinner in the oven. For a young child, the purpose of a walk is to encounter the universe, stimulate their senses, and develop neural connections in their brains (aka knowledge and skills). It's not that children won't focus on an end goal, it's that they can't. They lack the neurowiring to avoid distractions.

In terms of learning, this is great news. It means that children are open to every possibility. Take a toddler for a walk and every puddle, insect, weed, and piece of litter is fascinating and requires exploration. Toddlers simply can't hold in their heads that there is a higher purpose to a walk even if it is something that a moment ago they really wanted to do, such as getting to the park. Park? What park? Look at that shiny wrapper blowing along the ground!

That openness to distraction is brilliant for learning about every nook and cranny of a universe that children are still trying to figure out. Children's innate curiosity helps them to build their brains. Chasing that shiny wrapper, picking it up, listening to it crackle—these little moments create intelligence and creativity.

But those moments are lost if a parent in efficiency mode won't slow down to let their child chase that wrapper. Or jump in that puddle. Or prod those leaves with a stick. If we get too fixed on getting to the shop quickly, to buy the milk, to get home, to put the dinner on in time for clearing up before bedtime, then it's easy to interpret that shiny wrapper as unnecessary and our children as time-wasters (or worse, annoyances). Hurrying to get things done, we pull in the opposite direction from our children with the result that no one's needs are met and everyone feels frustrated or, worse, miserable.

"Too much efficiency thinking outside work can really get in the way."

THINKING POINT

List the skills and strengths you need to be good at your job. Then list the skills and strengths you think you need to be a good parent. Which skills and strengths do you think your child would say make a good parent? Check your assumptions by asking your child to list the top ten qualities that make a great mom/dad. (If they are little, they can draw a picture of the best mom/dad in the world and talk you through it.)

Parenting Is About Process Not Outcomes

Another way of thinking about this dichotomy is the difference between prioritizing process and prioritizing outcomes. Efficiency thinking prioritizes outcomes. Getting things done. Meeting targets. Ticking off the to-do list. Fitting more things into the day. All essential skills for modern working life.

When it comes to running a family, a bit of efficiency thinking can definitely be useful. Modern parenting involves heaps of organizing and logistics. When you walk in the door at home, your to-do list doesn't disappear, it just gets replaced by a different one—those million other jobs that need completing in your second shift. There's a meal to prepare, sandwiches to make, bags to pack, clothes to fold, hair to wash, gym clothes to find, stories to read, phone calls to make, food to order, birthday parties to organize. . . . It's an unending list. And some efficiency thinking will definitely help you through it. But getting stuck in efficiency mode is a trap. Because when we focus too much on end goals, we miss the moments. And in parenting, the moments are the real point.

When our minds are fixed on outcomes, we get easily frustrated when children don't meet those outcomes well enough or quickly enough—whether that's going to bed by 8:30 p.m., learning to read, or getting to the theme park on time. We get annoyed with them because they can't identify a word they read just yesterday. We argue with them for not doing their homework well enough. We shout at them for being slow to put on their shoes and get in the car so we can beat the lines and have a "fun family day out!"

By continually rushing children toward an outcome, we risk losing the moment we are in. And we miss the point. Being shouted at to get somewhere quickly in order to have fun is not fun. Learning to read happens through lots of enjoyable reading experiences, not by dreading each day's book in case you don't get it right enough. Parenting has an "ing" on it because it is a process, not a project to be completed. It is made up of a sequence of moments. We never really know whether we've got it right because the point is the moments themselves—there is no finishing line.

So don't let your work head take over and fool you otherwise.

HOW TO SWITCH FROM WORK MODE TO PARENT MODE

Avoiding getting stuck in efficiency thinking means learning to bridge two different personae: work mode and parent mode. To do that, you'll need to develop some habits that cue your body and brain into transitioning between your work and home skill sets. Good transition routines between work and home can be the difference between starting the evening ready to snap and walking into the house relaxed and resourced for the family evening ahead.

Good transition routines help working parents to

- park work worries and thoughts until the next day,
- deprioritize efficiency thinking,
- refocus on softer skills, and
- arrive home ready for the joys and challenges of a family evening.

The aim is to help you to stand down your efficiency thinking and crank up your softer parenting skills, such as empathy, curiosity, and playfulness. Investing some time developing transition routines that work for you makes positive parenting as a working parent much easier. Here are a few suggestions to help you switch from work mode to parent mode.

Don't Arrive Home Hungry or Thirsty

Being hungry or thirsty makes even the best of us cranky and more likely to snap. If you were too busy to eat or drink enough at work, be sure to pick up some water and a healthy snack on the way home. It's worth taking an extra five minutes to rebalance physically so that you don't start your parenting shift completely drained of energy. Paying attention to your own physical needs is essential if you are going to have the resources to respond to the demands of young (and inherently unreasonable) children.

Change Your Thoughts

It is hard to disengage from efficiency thinking if your head is full of work. So you need to find a way to let go of those work thoughts. Rather than scrolling through endless emails on the train home, try immersing yourself in a novel to distract from work thoughts (opt for gripping narratives that take you into their world completely). Audiobooks are great if you are driving. Or try listening to a funny podcast on your phone.

If distraction strategies don't work, or if your head is swirling with unfinished tasks, look for a strategy that will help you park those work thoughts until the next day. Grab a notebook (or electronic equivalent) and write down all the work stuff that is in your head. Then fold up your list and put it in your bag (or schedule your notes to pop up the next morning on your way to work). Once you know your thoughts have been captured and won't be lost, you shouldn't feel the need to think about them so much.

Trigger Positive Emotions

You can help yourself to trigger positive emotions by carrying with you a photo of your children or a drawing by your child. Something that gives you a fuzzy feeling when you look at it. Take it out when you are on the train or after you park the car and look at it for a few minutes. Conjure up your child's face, breathe, and let the love flow through you. Allow those fuzzy feelings to sweep through you and do their work. Tapping into positive emotions associated with our children can transport us straight into positive parent mode, energized and ready to connect with our children when we get home.

Find Something to Be Grateful for

Efficiency thinking works on a deficit model. It focuses our mind on what needs to be done and what hasn't yet been achieved. It leaves us dissatisfied, holding out the possibility of satisfaction only once we have reached the end goal. Focusing your thoughts on good things that have already happened is a great antidote to this. Close your eyes on your train journey home and compose a thank-you letter to your child in your head. Or make a mental list of all the things you are grateful for that your child has done or that he has brought into your life.

Deal with Stress

Stress makes us more judgmental and less likely to connect emotionally with our children. Too much stress damages parent–child relationships. So deal with your stress before you walk in the door. Take a few minutes on the way home to close your eyes and breathe deeply and slowly. Take a deep breath through your nose then exhale slowly through your mouth for a count of five. Sit on that bench around the corner from your home for one minute and just breathe. Then smile and feel your brain release the feel-good chemicals that come with smiling. Find a stress-relief moment that works for you and use it on the way home.

Practicing mindfulness is a great way to stop rushing and be present in the moment rather than three steps ahead—exactly what you'll need for stepping out of efficiency mode. Mindfulness involves bringing our attention to whatever is going on in this exact moment both inside and outside of ourselves. Gradually, through practice, we can train ourselves to become more aware of our thoughts and emotions and less controlled by them. Simply sitting and paying attention to physical sensations—sounds, smells, touch—can help to bring us into a calmer and more present state. While you are sitting on that bench, close your eyes and identify five things you can hear, three things you can smell, and one thing you can feel through your skin. Or download an app on your phone for guided mindfulness meditations you can use on the bus journey home.

Exercise can be a great stress reliever too, so try to build it into your journey. Can you bike rather than drive? Or just get off the bus a couple of stops early to walk? Yes, that will take a few minutes longer, but prioritizing arriving home in a good mood over saving a few minutes is exactly the reversal of efficiency thinking we are trying to achieve!

Pay Attention to the Kids as Soon as You Can

You know the kids are probably going to want a piece of you as soon as they see you. So accept that and don't try to do anything else for the first fifteen minutes. If you have little ones who are already at home when you walk in, sit down and give them your full attention. If you are sitting still and available to them, they are less likely to feel the need to fight for your attention. And once the connection has been reestablished, they will be much happier to let you disappear for a few moments to get changed, start dinner, or do whatever you need to do.

If you are picking your children up from childcare, try not to rush them straight into the journey home. Take a few minutes to be still and give them your attention. I know you have a hundred urgent reasons to get through the pick-up as quickly as possible ("What about dinner? The kids are hungry, I need to get them home!"), but that's exactly the time-saving efficiency thinking that you need to dial down a little if you are going to switch out of work mode. Rather than hurrying everyone through the pick-up as quickly as possible, take five minutes to do nothing but pay them your full attention so you can retune to child mode. If you can't hang around in situ, take a drink and a snack and find a bench nearby where you can sit for five minutes before heading off.

THINKING POINT

What mindset are you in when you first reunite with your child(ren) after work? How do you feel physically? What thoughts are in your head? What do you do in that first ten minutes when you reunite?

What mindset would you like to be in? How would you like to feel physically? Close your eyes and visualize how the reunion might feel if you were in that different mindset. How might the first ten minutes look if you were in a different frame of mind?

Change Your Clothes

It sounds really simple, but most of us wear a uniform to work of one sort or another—a suit and tie, a smart blouse, or a skirt and heels. Changing out of your work clothes once you get home is a great psychological trick to help your brain switch into parent mode. Your home clothes are probably comfier too and so are easier to relax in. All the better for playing and cuddling!

Play with Your Children

Play is a brilliant way to switch modes and connect with your children. You might not be able to do it straight away, and I know you have a million things to do, but try to dedicate fifteen minutes in your evening routine to playing with your children. Wholeheartedly. Playing while your brain is on work, dinner, or other things is no good here—try to immerse yourself fully in play and actually have fun. Just for fifteen minutes. Forget you are a grown-up. To hell with logical thinking, quotas, and targets. In play mode, dinosaurs live in farms and get beaten up by sheep! So horse around. Kick a ball. Play a manic driving game with your tween on the computer. Or just take the kids outside with a blanket to lie down and find pictures in the stars. Be in the moment, tune in to your child's playfulness, step out of manic work mode, and play.

Disrupt Negative Routines

Do the kids start bickering the minute you get home? Do they kick off in the car on the way back from the childminder? Are there tears and tantrums within ten minutes of you getting home? If so, it's probably a bid for attention. Sometimes we can get stuck in a bad transition routine and everyone gets into a negative habit that seems to repeat each day.

Don't keep doing the same things if your work–home transition isn't working. Get disruptive and try something new. Try talking to the kids on the phone before you arrive (video calling is ideal with younger children!). If you are picking them up, take a detour to see the ducks before you head home. Or grab some sandwiches on the way back from work and go straight to the park for a picnic dinner. If it's winter, go for a surprise walk in the dark with wellies and torches, or drink hot chocolates in a local café as a treat before heading home. Or try a big one-off disruption to break a negative pattern—why not surprise the children and bundle everyone into the car after work and go bowling for half an hour?

No, it isn't an efficient use of time. And yes, it will disrupt their routine. But when you are stuck in a negative rut, sticking rigidly to the same routine is not the answer. (Just because something theoretically should be working is no good reason to keep at it when it obviously isn't.) If you can disrupt a negative routine even just a few times, it creates space for a new mode of interacting with each other to get established.

Of course, you won't be able to spend every minute of your family life in go-slower mode. Family life has deadlines too. There will always be times when getting from A to B actually is the priority—whether that's getting to a doctor's appointment or not missing the school bell. A little bit of efficiency thinking can certainly oil the wheels of family life. But if you never slow down and chase that shiny wrapper, you'll miss a precious opportunity to build quality family relationships and create a family life you enjoy being part of.

> **"Being able to consciously transition out of manic mode and dial down your goal-focused thinking opens the door to a set of precious parental strengths and meaningful interactions."**

ACTION POINTS

- Choose three ideas to try out in the next fortnight of new things to do on your journey back from work that might help to park your work thoughts and calm yourself physically.
- Next time you are just about to see your child(ren) after work, pause for two minutes. Close your eyes and imagine their face(s) in as much detail as possible. Once you can see them in your mind's eye, smile.

3

Tuning in and Getting Connected

How we think about our role as parents makes a big difference to how we approach parenting. When we are stuck in "get-the-job-done" efficiency thinking mode, we tend to focus on all the tasks that need completing before bedtime: feeding, washing, laundry, spellings, reading, telling off, chasing down lost gym clothes (my son lost his gym clothes a lot, can you tell?!). . . . Even thinking about it all is stressful! That mental load of stuff to do weighs heavily on our home life. Evenings can become something to be gotten through rather than time to be enjoyed with the people we love.

But families are made up of relationships, not tasks. One of the biggest dangers of getting stuck in task-focused thinking is that it interferes with how we connect with our children. When we are in work mode, we automatically push toward an outcome: "My child is crying, my task is to remove their distress"; "My child is in a difficult situation, my task is to dispense advice"; "My child has done something silly, my task is to admonish them." We close down our communications with our children very quickly in our rush toward that end goal. And we don't always pause to listen and meet our children's need for a connection rather than a solution.

If we reframe our thinking about parenting away from a list of activities to be completed or a project to be undertaken and see our job as parents in terms of building a relationship with our child, that opens the door to a very different dynamic. Good relationships are mutual and respectful, built on acceptance, curiosity, empathy, and enjoying each other's company.

Building a relationship isn't a job that can be ticked off a weekend to-do list. It's about small choices that we make on a day-to-day level. It's about chatting, laughing, and slowing down for a few minutes to listen when our child has something to say—really listen with all our attention, not just half our brains. Because it's through listening that we connect with our children on a deeper level and get to know them. Building relationships is not about large quantities of time, it's about quality moments. It's not day trips or outings to the zoo that create connection, it's everyday interactions.

WHAT ARE RELATIONSHIPS MADE OF?

When I ask parents what makes a good relationship, the answers usually contain words like "trust," "communication," and "respect." Those certainly are ingredients of a good relationship. But how do trust or respect come about? They come from little moments, from small interactions. A good relationship evolves from interactions between two people that, through repetition, become a pattern. That pattern makes us feel a particular way and leads us to expect that future interactions will also go a certain way. If it is a good relationship, for example, we feel safe and supported, whereas bad relationships make us feel threatened and on edge, and we are much more likely to interpret the other person's actions as ill intentioned. Relationships are built from moments that settle into a pattern and that add up to a greater whole.

Babies start to build a relationship with their caregivers from the moment they are born. It's a simple relationship that says, "I have a need, please meet it." To start with, their method of communication is blunt and imprecise: they cry. New parents are left to guess which need that particular cry relates to by scrambling through a checklist (gas? hunger? wet? cold? hot?) until they stumble on an action that seems to soothe. But slowly, through a (somewhat grueling!) repetition of that interaction, we learn to distinguish a baby's different needs. And babies learn how to give different signals for different circumstances. If their needs are met often enough, infants develop a template (an "inner working model") of their relationship with us in which they feel safe and secure and generally expect that their needs will be met.

This early attachment process has often been overinterpreted. It has been wielded as a guilt stick for beating up working mothers and as a handy excuse for excluding fathers from childcare. There is nothing in attachment theory that says a young child requires a single, devoted female parent on hand to meet their every need at the earliest opportunity in order to guarantee their healthy emotional development. Yet this idealized image of perfect mother–child bonding is so pervasive that many of us have internalized the belief that it would be better for children if their mothers were at home and that moms going to work is a shoddy compromise. Children certainly do need attachments in order to thrive, and the more secure the better, but there is no evidence that a single always-present female attachment figure is essential for a child's healthy development. And there is plenty of evidence that having a variety of caregivers in children's lives with whom they can form secure attachments is beneficial.

Attachment theories have also been misused to suggest that in order to promote a secure attachment and be "good" parents we need to be 100 percent available and responsive to young children's needs. (Another guilt stick with which to beat absent working parents!) In fact, a strong attachment is not created by parents jumping to meet an infant's every need. Creating a healthy connection with children actually means knowing them well enough that we can identify the need being expressed, but that we also have a good measure of their capacity to tolerate that need or discomfort so that we can leave them to gradually learn to manage their own needs and regulate their own feelings independently without our help. That means recognizing the difference between "I'm really frightened, I need this to stop right now" and "I feel a bit uneasy and I'm not sure if I can cope with it" and responding accordingly. A good connection involves putting your own preoccupations to one side, learning to tune in to your unique child, getting it right often enough (not always), and repairing through cuddles and closeness when you don't.

Attachment has also been portrayed as a once-only opportunity: "You'd better get it right in the first year because if you get it wrong, your child is doomed!" Certainly rapid developments in babies' brains do make the first year of life a crucial and vulnerable period. But although infants develop an inner working model for future relationships in their early attachment patterns, it is too easy to regard attachment as fixed forever. Our relationship template is refined and developed throughout childhood, through different relationships, and, indeed, throughout our lives. Each moment, each interaction, informs the relationship pattern we build with our children. Building a good relationship with your child is an ongoing process of learning to recognize their changing needs and working out how best to meet them. Crucially, that means mastering the work/parent switch in order to prioritize the process of communication rather than its outcomes and really listening to what our children have to say.

WHEN TO TALK AND HOW TO LISTEN

Parents often see it as our job in a conversation to impart knowledge to children or to direct their actions. We think that we know best (to be fair, we often do!). But if we are short on time and convinced we know best, it's tempting not to waste time listening to children and just wade straight in with our pronouncements. We go nuts because our child has done something foolish ("I can't believe you left it out in the rain! That was your sister's special toy and now you've ruined it!"). Or we prioritize solutions rather than taking time to help our child understand the situation ("Go and say sorry and give her one of your toys"). We react and direct, we don't listen.

I mean *really* listen. Not just to glean the key facts. I mean buttoning up our mouths, putting judgments to one side, and being curious about what our child is saying and how they are saying it, listening to understand not just the words but also the emotions and intentions. When we don't listen in this active way, we often jump to conclusions that aren't right. We are quick to attribute blame. Or we offer solutions that our child can't connect with because they haven't gone through the process of understanding the problem for themselves. By jumping to an endpoint, we fundamentally mistake the purpose of communication with children.

At work, when colleagues come to talk to us, they are usually looking for a definite answer or a solution to a problem. Frequently, they want an answer right here, right now. ASAP! At work we are conditioned to become solution-focused missiles. When children interact with us, however, the purpose of that communication is a little different. Children are not looking to us for an answer, they are trying to understand the question. Children are discovering themselves and the world around them through their interactions with us. By connecting with us, they are looking to understand the situation they are in and the emotion they are feeling (and to know that it's OK to feel that way). They don't need to be given an answer, they need to be helped to understand the situation and their feelings about it well enough that they can find their own answer. And that requires us to put our suggestions and judgments to one side and be with our children in their moment.

Learning to pause, be curious, and hold back suggestions is hard when you are time poor, especially when the solution looks obvious, your child is distressed, or the issue is something worrying. But by short-circuiting straight to solutions, we miss the real point of listening—seeing the world from our child's point of view. Picture this:

Parent: What's the matter? Why are you upset?

Daughter: Ellie was nasty to me.

Parent: What did she do?

Daughter: She said I have hair like a bear.

A pretty familiar scenario, yes? As a parent there are two ways we can go with this conversation. One of them will hand her a ready-made solution quickly and efficiently. And one of them will create connection and empower our daughter to manage her emotions and relationships independently going forward.

Option 1:

Parent: Don't be silly. You have lovely hair. Just ignore her/tell the teacher/don't play with her anymore/tell her she's an idiot.* (*delete according to parental values/preference)

Option 2:

Parent: That wasn't very nice. How did that make you feel?

Daughter: I feel sad.

Parent: I can understand that. It's not nice when people say horrible things. Why do you think she said it?

Daughter: Because I have curly hair and it won't stay in a braid.

Parent: Is there something wrong with having curly hair?

Daughter: Ellie has straight hair and she wears it in a braid but I can't do that because mine isn't long enough.

Parent: So you think she said it because your hair is different from hers?

Daughter: I guess so.

Parent: Is there anything wrong with being different?

Daughter: No. But she said it to be unkind.

Parent: She said it deliberately to be unkind. I'm not surprised you're upset. That's not nice.

Daughter: No.

Parent: Have you got any ideas what you could do about it?

Daughter: If she does it again, I'm going to tell her to stop being unkind and I'm going to play with Jenna instead.

Parent: That sounds like a good plan. You look like you're feeling a little bit better now.

Daughter: Yes. But I'd like another cuddle.

Parent: OK, it's a deal.

The second option is one hundred times better both in terms of children's social-emotional development and in creating a positive relationship. In Option 2, the parent is accepting, curious, and empathetic. The child's concerns and emotions are not dismissed or judged. The parent asks clarifying questions to learn more rather than making pronouncements. And the parent acknowledges that it's not nice having that feeling. In Option 2, the child goes away feeling that her need for comfort through connection has been met and with a better understanding of her experience. She has also met a developmental need to learn independent problem solving and self-regulation, though she is possibly less aware of that! In Option 1, the parent goes away feeling that they have met their need to solve the issue quickly and efficiently by dispensing advice (and who knows what the child felt—the parent didn't stop to find out).

The problem for working parents is clearly that the Option 2 takes longer. "You must be kidding, I don't have time for that!" But the time difference is actually minimal (Option 1 takes about four seconds while Option 2 is one minute). You won't be able to choose Option 2 in every single conversation, but that's OK—you don't have to. A strong connection doesn't mean getting it right every single time. Just often enough (research would suggest about 30 percent getting it right is "good enough" if you need a figure!). When you are a rushing parent with little time to spare, you will sometimes get it wrong. It's very easy to dismiss children's thoughts and feelings (after all, they are frequently illogical, out of proportion, or just plain silly!) and jump in with assumptions and solutions. It doesn't make you a terrible parent and it won't mean your children are doomed. Just try to catch yourself doing it, forgive yourself, and put yourself back on track. If you miss a moment, go back to it: "You know when you were talking about Ellie being mean about your hair? I thought about it and I don't think I said the right things. You seemed upset and I don't think I listened properly. How are you feeling about it now?" Simply being alert to the potential of moments to build connection will help us find those moments when we can get it right a little more often.

QUICK WAYS TO CONNECT

Tuning in and getting connected is all about how you use the minutes, not the days. It's as much about those little bits of time around the edges of work as it is about holidays and day trips. For working parents, that means turning off your "parenting as a goal focused project" thinking and being in the moment with your child so that you can make the most of little bits of time to build rapport and create a positive dynamic. There are lots of things that parents can do to develop a positive relationship with children that fit around the working day and don't take up a lot of time—small actions that can make a really big difference.

Play Together

In those bits of time that you do have with your child, make sure it's not all productive time. Have some downtime. Give a bit of space for things to happen. Carve out pockets of playfulness, hanging out, and being affectionate. Small frequent amounts of time are the building blocks for a good relationship: ten minutes kicking a ball around or half an hour when you switch off your phones and watch something funny together (my tween and I majorly bonded over episodes of *Modern Family*!). Aim for "little and often" good times rather than occasional whole days.

Relationships thrive on joint positive experiences, so do things with your child that you both enjoy. When we are really enjoying ourselves, we communicate that in all our facial expressions and body language. Equally, when we aren't really enjoying an activity, that leaks out too. So if jigsaws are your personal hell, avoid them. Choose things to do with your child that you genuinely enjoy and that fit into the small pockets of time you have available. Aim for fifteen minutes a day playing with your child wholeheartedly (not with your mind on other things!). If you have more than one child and they have different interests, you might not manage fifteen minutes with each child every day, but do what you can. And try to carve out longer periods of play time for each child at some point during the week.

This is not the type of play where the parent is in charge, where you tell your child what to do or control the activity. I mean joint and reciprocal play where you are both equal partners and both build on each other's ideas. Like children do together. The type of play where you tune into each other, suspend your typical roles, and have real fun. It might be running around play, or dressing up role-play, or constructing something together, or a game of Snap!, or a car racing game on the console—it doesn't really matter, and it doesn't have to take long. What matters is that you are both engaged and enjoying it. Immersed in play, we are in a state of flow, totally absorbed in the moment in a way that not only builds relationships, it boosts everyone's well-being like a shot of vitamin C.

Be Affectionate

Physical affection plays a key role in forming secure bonds between children and parents. A hug, a kiss, or a ruffle of their hair—these convey acceptance and closeness and make children feel wanted, loved, and secure. Growing up in a warm and affectionate environment is directly linked to positive long-term outcomes for children. For very young children, being held in a loving and gentle way boosts their immune system. The comforting touch of a parent gets hardwired into babies' brains, making them better able to regulate emotions and stress throughout their childhoods. Physical affection promotes self-esteem, reduces anxiety, and builds trust.

Being affectionate also releases feel-good chemicals in parents, reducing our stress levels and making us feel calmer. And a calm parent is a happy parent. As they get older, children might not want you cuddling them in front of their friends (I can't tell you how jealous I am of those of you who have little ones, now that my big teens no longer fit in my lap!). If they don't want to hold hands or be hugged in public, a rub on their back or just a smile or a wink does make a difference and keeps you feeling close.

Be Interruptible

Remember that relationships are built out of moments. So when you are with your child, be available to them. If you are doing other things (unavoidable stuff like laundry and making dinner), try to be interruptible. Prioritize those "turn to" moments when your child comes to show you a picture or ask a question ("Daddy, how does the moon stay in the sky?"). These are the moments when your child is asking you to engage, when they are reaching out for connection.

Stop what you are doing and pay attention to them. Just for a few minutes. Engage with them. Answer their questions (don't just tell them to Google it). Look at what they are showing you. Laugh at their joke. Just for a few minutes (yes, I know you are really busy). Then send them off on a mission to do/find/play with something. And you can get back to whatever you were doing.

Working parents have a hundred things to do every evening. But think of the message it sends to our children if we are always too busy to stop for a moment. "Not now, I'm busy. I'm doing the washing up, I'll look at it later." Our attention conveys value. What we pay attention to is what matters to us. What does it say to our children if everything is always more important than stopping and listening to them? It won't be possible every single time but, unless the dinner is actually going to burn, try to stop for a few moments, pay them the attention they are asking for, and then send them on their way to do something or find something.

Remember, that moment will only come once; the washing up will wait. So learn to switch out of efficiency mode and seize those little moments to establish connection.

THINKING POINT

How often do you say to your child(ren): "Not now, I'm busy"? What are you doing in those moments? What would the impact be if you stopped for two minutes?

Create Special Traditions

Setting up special traditions can help you become an important part of your child's routine even when you have very limited time. Small regular events are great—like mom always making pancakes on Sundays or dad taking the kids swimming on Saturday mornings. Or it might be bigger, less frequent events like trips to the same campsite every summer or reading the same book every Christmas Eve. Even tiny things like saying "Goodnight" using the same phrase every bedtime or telling the same joke every time you go to visit grandma strengthens bonds and stitches together diverse moments into a sense of continuity.

> **"Rituals and traditions are really useful because they confer significance on your time together."**

Traditions occupy more space emotionally and psychologically than the amount of time they actually take up. You can talk about traditions in between times and anticipate the next one ("I'm really looking forward to going swimming with you on Saturday"). You can build traditions into shared memories ("Do you remember that guy in the Beano shorts who fell in the pool?!"). Traditions feel special to the people participating in them. So if you don't have much time with your children, doing the same thing together again and again can provide a thread that pulls together all your separate moments into a stronger fabric.

As well as bonding families together, traditions and rituals give children a sense of belonging. They mark out your family identity, your unique family culture. And they help parents and children build up a happy memory bank, which is really positive for children's emotional resilience. Memories are portable, we store them in our heads, and they are always with us. You can revisit a happy memory at any time to make yourself happy in the present. So having a bank of good memories is a bit like creating a happy place in children's heads (and yours)—everyone in the family can revisit those memories. Telling stories about things you have done together as a family ("Do you remember when dad dressed up as Queen Victoria?") and revisiting past rituals ("Do you remember when you were little and we used to wave at that windmill and call it Mr. Slowcoach?") fixes those memories in your children's heads and strengthens connections.

THINKING POINT

Which traditions and rituals do you have that create regular and significant moments for you and your child? Check your assumptions by asking your child about their favorite time of the day/week and about their favorite memories from the past year.

Connect Even If You're Not There

If you can't be with your child for whatever reason, chatting by phone or video call is a great alternative. It lets them know that you are thinking about them even when you aren't present. If you have to be away from your child, either regularly or as a one-off, find ways to reach across the absence to let them know how important they are to you. You could join them for their bedtime story via video call or even read a book to them via FaceTime.

And if you can't be there for a special moment, plan ahead. Let your child know that you are with them in spirit: send them a thoughtful text or a funny picture of you, pre-prepare a note for their lunchbox, or hide a surprise somewhere in the house and leave them a clue where to find it. (It doesn't have to be anything expensive, just an "IOU a cuddle" note stuck to their favorite teddy!) You don't always have to be physically present to have meaningful moments—find ways to communicate and stay present for your children even when you are absent.

What Did You Do Today? Nothing!

"But I try to connect and I don't get anything back!" I wish I had a penny for every time I asked my son, "How was school today?" and got the answer, "Fine." Children seldom like to talk on demand (and seldom like to be quiet when talking is unwelcome!). When parents ask direct questions, children often clam up and their shutters come crashing down—especially if their parents are in the habit of falling into critical behavior police mode a bit too often (remember those parenting holes?). "What did you do at school today?" is interpreted as "What did you do today that I need to know about?" And children will often give no answer rather than risk a wrong answer or one that might get them into unforeseen trouble.

So here's a quick idea to try out. You lead the way. You do the talking. Tell them about your day. Talk about the weather, the sunset, what you had for lunch, the guy you saw falling over on the way to work—anything. Just chat and see where it leads you. Make it interesting and children are often much more likely to jump into a conversation. A chatty, indirect approach often gets kids talking. Talk about yourself, the neighbors, family members, the dog, their friends. Talk about the characters in their favorite TV program (while watching it together). Children will often engage enthusiastically in conversations about other people (real or fictional) and in a way that really helps you to stay in touch with their thought processes and opinions. Plot lines in films are a great launch pad for talking about friendship issues. Celebrity gossip is great for talking about social and emotional issues. If you want to talk about effort and reward, talk about sports. Be indirect and you will often get a lot more back from your child (and learn a lot more about them).

Try not to use every conversation as a mechanism for giving information (or pressing your kids for information). If you walk in the door after work with an agenda of stuff you need to talk to your child about, it seldom goes well. Talk about meaningless stuff and the important stuff is much more likely to find the right moment to come out.

> **"Those little nuggets of communication are the threads that bond you together."**

Children often open up when talking side by side rather than face to face. So make the most of car journeys to chat about everything and anything.

One parent I know used to go for "car chats" with her ten-year-old son when confrontation was brewing as a way of talking about difficult things without arguing. Sometimes you'll find your child tells you things in a casual chat on the drive to their cello lesson that wouldn't have come out otherwise. Or try chatting side by side on the sofa. Or cuddle up for a bedtime chat.

Parenting will always have its rocky moments. Children don't usually come to us and tell us in their sweetest voices that they are feeling angry, tired, or scared. Their communications are more oblique and they often express themselves through their behavior. But having a positive connection with your child makes it a lot easier to get through those sticky moments. Good relationships give back more than we put in. They bring joy, intimacy, and emotional sustenance—exactly what hard-working parents need to keep going.

ACTION POINTS

- The next time your child comes to you with a problem, don't offer a solution. Ask questions to help clarify the problem. If it is an emotional issue, name the emotion they are having. Re-present the clarified problem back to your child ("So, the problem is . . .") and ask if they have any ideas what to do about it.
- Pick a chatty moment, such as in the car, over dinner, or when you are snuggled up for a bedtime story, and tell your child something about your day. Something you enjoyed or something strange, funny, or interesting that happened that day.

4

Making Space for Playfulness

Playfulness is the opposite of work mode efficiency thinking. It is something we do for joy and pleasure, not as a means to an end goal. For stressed-out working parents stretched too thin by too many tasks, a spirit of playfulness has the potential to jolt us right out of our battle stations mode and make everything worthwhile. As long as we make space for it. For children, play is their purpose. It is the driving force that creates their intelligence and makes childhood magical. Playfulness is an essential ingredient in happy families. Children need it and adults need it. If you take the play out of parenting, all you are left with is drudgery.

"But we are too busy, we don't have time for play! It doesn't accomplish anything, there are too many other things to do. We have responsibilities. Play is messy, inconvenient, and unproductive!" When our priority is getting things done, play is the first thing we ditch. Playfulness gets squeezed out by the sheer weight of our mental load. It is forced out by electronic gadgets, overscheduling, our reluctance to let children take risks, and our sheer lack of energy. Yet ironically, playfulness is the exact antidote to the efficiency-based thinking that tells us we don't have enough time for play.

"What about all those kid-centric activities we do every weekend?" I hear you ask. Those petting farms and football matches and medieval castles? Well, are they actually playful? I'll bet you the only time your kids were playful on your last visit to a castle was when you sat down on the lawn outside to eat sandwiches and they ran around pretending to be knights and princesses. And I'll also bet that if they ran around inside the castle, they were told to stop and walk because being playful in public places is only allowed within strict confines—like dressing up in an educationally relevant peasant's costume or pretending to eat fake medieval food. (And your kids didn't linger on those activities, did they? Because they weren't actually that fun.)

Children's play is increasingly being restricted to specific times and specialized places. Children spend more time indoors and in supervised activities. Adults take children to designated places to "do" play—we give up our "free" time to take them to clubs, theme parks, petting zoos, and soft play centers, where their play is structured, contained, and mediated. Children's play has become a commodity we buy. Parents obsess about making sure our children are attending all the right clubs and participating in "beneficial" extracurricular activities. It can feel as if we are letting them down if they aren't simultaneously playing several sports, learning a musical instrument, and attending French/chess/drama clubs. But let our children play outside unsupervised in the street? No. That we no longer do. Increases in traffic, the rise of tech, and concerns about safety mean that genuinely free, unstructured outdoor play is something children experience much less now.

Cajoling a herd of children in and out of the car to clubs, rehearsals, and matches doesn't add up to a fun family life. Working parents are so overloaded with a sense of responsibility that we are, ironically, too busy and too tired for the antidote. Play is the pixie dust that makes our lives feel lighter. Playfulness fuels children's development, makes parenting enjoyable, strengthens family bonds, and boosts everyone's well-being. Creating more space for playfulness will give you room to breathe, relax, laugh a little more (and shout a little less), and enjoy being a member of your family.

PLAY BUILDS CHILDREN'S BRAINS

Play is the fuel behind children's development. It is the most important thing a child can do. Play is how children build their brains and bodies and learn about the universe. It is through play that children come to understand people and relationships and develop the core skills to function in the world. Play is the work of childhood.

Young children don't learn about the world by sitting back and contemplating it. Young children learn about the world through physical and sensory experiences: touching, tasting, watching, throwing, jumping, and climbing into things. If you hold a ball up in front of a five-year-old and ask what will happen when you let it go, he will tell you that the ball will drop to the ground. (And he'll probably give you a quizzical look for asking such a dumb question.) That five-year-old has a clear functional understanding of gravity. But he didn't learn it through anyone explaining gravity to him. (To be honest, I don't think I could explain gravity very well if I tried!) How did he learn it? By throwing things, dropping things, and falling over. He learned it through play.

Good-quality play builds children's intelligence. When babies are born, their brains are full of neurons, like long pieces of string. By interacting with their environment through playful experiences, these brain cells get connected together into pathways and networks that store knowledge and skills. Play literally builds brains. Children need their opportunities for play to be as wide and as varied as possible so they can interact with their environment in many different ways in order to maximize those neural connections. The more varied their play, the more flexible and adaptive their brains become. And play builds physical skills too. Interacting playfully with the environment builds strong muscles and helps children develop their motor skills (good for running around and kicking a ball) and their dexterity (essential for small, controlled movements like writing).

Children need a rich and balanced play diet in order to acquire all the skills and knowledge needed to be resourceful and successful adults. They need structured play (where they learn to follow rules, listen to a leader, and practice in order to get better) and team games (where they learn strategy, cooperation, and social and emotional skills), and they need time playing with parents, playing alone, playing with younger children, playing in mixed age groups, and playing competitive games (that they sometimes win and sometimes lose). But they especially need free play.

Free play is that type of play that is child led and child driven. It is what children do when nobody tells them what to do (and when there is no screen available). Free play has no externally set goals and is not structured by adults. It is self-directed and fueled entirely by children's imagination and enjoyment, like building a den out of sofa cushions and then deciding it's actually a zoo and getting out all the toy animals that then climb the sofa cushion mountains and traverse the forest of potted plants to reach the city of shoes. But, oh no, the city is defended by giant doll monsters! Free play is what children do when they are left to their own devices. It's how they learn that sticks float, stones sink, and water flows (and soaks through socks). There is no extracurricular club that does for child development what free play can do. It costs nothing, requires minimal effort from parents, and feels brilliant.

WHY PLAY IS GOOD FOR PARENTS TOO

Many working parents fall into the trap of thinking that being hyperorganized in our family lives makes us effective as parents. We race through tasks, ticking off our to-do list, creating a sense of accomplishment. "Look! I've managed to get it all done! My kids are clothed and fed and at school on time! Ethan got Player of the Week and Amy passed her Level 1. I even played a bit of Lego with Jack this week—I may be a wreck but I'm succeeding as a parent!" But without the pixie dust of playfulness, a hyperscheduled ultra-organized life is just hard work.

Creating space for playfulness is more than just putting a tick in the fun mom/dad box. It's good for us. Being genuinely playful with children taps straight into the five essential elements of well-being:

1. Positive emotions.
2. Engagement.
3. Meaning.
4. Positive relationships.
5. A sense of accomplishment.

Play is all about positive, pleasurable emotions—joy, zest, ebullience. (And if you aren't having those feelings while you are playing, you aren't being playful—you are just going through the motions.) Real playfulness involves being 100 percent in the moment and going with the flow. It is the epitome of mindfulness. When you watch children playing, it is impossible not to be struck by how completely absorbed they are by what they are doing. Being truly playful involves stepping into the moment and being totally engaged in the present. It is what psychologists call a state of "flow" in which we lose our self-consciousness and immerse ourselves in the moment. (If you want to feel the difference of truly immersed play, challenge your child to a game of Snap! and play to win.) Activities that induce flow are consistently linked to reduced stress and improved mental and emotional well-being. Being a fun parent is genuinely good for you!

THINKING POINT

When was the last time you felt truly playful and immersed in the present moment with your children? What could you do to re-create that moment a little more often? How would that impact you?

But play not only makes parenting more enjoyable, it also makes you feel like a better parent. It gives a greater meaning to everything you do as a parent. A to-do list approach to family life will always leave you feeling like you could be doing better because there will always be something left on the list that you haven't accomplished (and it will all need doing again tomorrow anyway). But when we enter into a spirit of playfulness with our children, we hit that sweet zone where the whole point of being with children is illuminated. This is what we became parents for. This is the feeling we remember from our childhoods. And that sense of meaning and happiness creates a greater sense of competence, a feeling that we are somehow on a deeper level getting it right as parents. (And I never ever had that feeling from doing the washing up!)

"Playing with your children strengthens your connection with them and deepens your understanding of them."

When children play together in imaginative play, they are simultaneously engaged in their own play but also alert and open to their play partners. They read each other's subtle signals and build on each other's ideas, navigating complex negotiations in which everyone spontaneously understands that the toy they are playing with is now a spade, not a frying pan. If you can suspend your adult self and be that equal play partner, even for short bursts, it not only helps you to destress, it also activates your work/parent switch and brings huge rewards in terms of building a positive relationship with your child. Playfulness requires you to tune in to your child, to read their mood and intentions and be on an equal level. It requires trust and creates a better understanding of each other. Being playful with children conveys acceptance—that you like them and enjoy them exactly the way they are, which is fantastic for building children's self-esteem. And parents receive the same in return.

Even when you don't join in, making space for playfulness has major benefits for working parents. Creating space for children's independent free play gives working parents much-needed time to relax. While your kids are collecting sticks to make an ants' castle, you can be sitting on a bench drinking in the sunshine. Or talking to a friend. Or reading a book. Or listening to a podcast. Or doing the vacuuming occasionally (if you absolutely must). Prioritizing play doesn't cost time, it gives back time. And well-being.

THINKING POINT

After every play activity you do with your child this week, rate how much you think your child enjoyed the experience and also how much you enjoyed it. Use a scoring method (10/10 for "the best time ever," 1/10 for "it was terrible").

If your enjoyment was 5 or under, think about what you could do to make that activity more enjoyable next time or plan an alternative activity to try out instead. You can check your assumptions by asking your child to do their own rating too.

FINDING ROOM FOR PLAY IN BUSY LIVES

Some adults are good at playing, others aren't. Lots of us lose touch with our childish play instincts and find it hard to suspend our adult selves. I used to get annoyed when the kids muddled up the dinosaurs and the farm animals (they're from different eras, for goodness sake!). Our efficiency work mode indoctrinates us into always working to a plan and we can find it hard to just go with the flow of anarchic play. Some parents find it hard to step outside our instructor role and be an equal play partner—we look for learning points in the activity and try to direct and control rather than following our child's lead and playing just for playing's sake.

If that's you, then I suggest you fake it at first. You'll get better at playing the more you do it. Pretend you are six. Step out of your parent role and regress. It might feel weird at first, but the more you do it the easier it gets and the more you'll enjoy it. Join in with whatever your child is already playing. If he is acting out a scene with action figures, grab another figure (or doll or animal or teddy) and join in the scene. Or just wait for your child's ideas and let him direct. Be sure to fully participate in his thinking rather than bringing your adult brain to organize the play. If an idea pops into your head that builds on the flow of the play, suggest it tentatively ("We could pretend to be giants who are attacking their world," "Shall we get the bricks and build a castle for them to live in?"), but be sure to follow, not to lead. If your child is short on ideas or just not used to you playing with him in this way, put something on to spark his curiosity (a hat, a scarf, an upturned pot on your head) and sit or lie on the floor next to him. Say something in a silly voice and see what happens. If time is short, set a timer on your phone so you don't have to watch the clock. Until that buzzer goes off, you are free to go with the flow and see where the play leads you. And if you don't like the flow of the game? Be disruptive, like a six-year-old would!

If you have really young children (up to three years old), spend some time observing them while they are playing. Watch closely, without stepping in. Observe how they interact with their environment and with other children. What skills are they practicing? What skills have they already mastered? Just sit back and reflect on their self-initiated play without trying to control or intervene. It's a powerful experience that really helps you understand where your child is developmentally and how they go about playing. It's also a great excuse for a cup of tea!

With older children, try not to always do activities where you are the expert. Seek out games where there is a more level playing field and you are not directing. Learning a new skill at the same time as your child is great—check out your local college or children's center for family learning opportunities. Or choose activities where there is an instructor in charge so parents can be genuine participants. If you have a whole afternoon to spare and have adventure-loving kids, high-adrenaline activities like forest high-ropes are brilliant for fun family team building—especially when the kids have to help their parents navigate an obstacle. Or try luck-based board games that the whole family can play—and that anyone can win. Or something quieter like coloring together (buy a coloring book each so you really get involved and are not tempted to direct what your child is doing!). Or helping your child with a Lego construction that neither of you has tackled before (if there are instructions, give them to your child to follow so they can be in charge). Take an interest in whatever interests your children and be their play partner, not their boss or their teacher. If you've got a tween who is permanently attached to a gadget or game, why not join in sometimes? That sense of equality in play (or being better than your parent at something!) can be a great relationship builder.

It's not always about joining in (I promise, I do know how busy you are!). Creating space for playfulness means sometimes, literally, just providing a space for children's imaginations to roam and leaving them to it. If you want to encourage free play, focus on providing an interesting environment. An interesting environment for a child is not necessarily one that is full of toys—fewer choices often lead to better play than a room full of toys. If your child gets bored, despite having millions of toys, put three-quarters of the toys away somewhere and rotate them every few weeks. Or swap them with friends or join a toy library. Children like novelty. Surprise your children with a box full of kitchen utensils and see what happens. Or a box full of old clothes they have never seen before. Then put them away again the next week before they can get bored of them. Focus on providing basic play materials that can be used in lots of different ways. The recycling box is a great place to start—add some scraps of fabric, pipe cleaners, and bulldog clips. Then let them get on with it while you get on with something else. (Or have a cup of tea—your choice!)

One of the biggest reasons that parents confine or restrict children's play is because it's messy. Cleaning up is just one more thing to do. And play can be loud and boisterous in a small home. If that's an issue, head outside as much as possible. Outdoor play in natural settings is fantastic for children's development. The outdoors is a sensory-rich environment for children—whether it's urban or rural, there are lots of things to look at, feel, smell, and hear. And it is constantly changing. Creatures appear and move around, the weather is different from one day to the next—there are puddles, shadows, mist, and wind. The opportunities for explorative learning are limitless. Go for a family walk and take it at your child's pace (so what if you only manage 100 yards?). Or just sit down in the park and let them roll around on the grass while you breathe for five minutes. Give them a shovel to make mud pies in the garden or some old clothes for building a scarecrow stuffed with leaves. Head to the woods and collect sticks to make a mini village for insects or go for a walk on the beach in rain boots in the winter. If you can't venture that far, just give them a piece of chalk and let them draw pictures on a wall outside—you can wash them off with a water pistol or plant sprayer. These are not only brain boosters for kids and a well-being boost for parents, this is also the stuff that happy memories are made of.

You may not have a big garden or a safe neighborhood, but all children need to connect with nature, to take their time pulling petals off flowers and watching flies clean their wings, to dig soil and collect stones, feel grass on their skin and bruise themselves rolling down hills. Challenge yourself to stop saying "No" so often. Let them get messy and create a bit of havoc. Let them deconstruct their toys to see how they work (and maybe not manage to put them back together again). Let them learn resilience through play by overcoming obstacles and managing their inevitable frustrations and disappointments. I promise you'll be doing more for their development than bullying them into practicing a violin that they absolutely hate.

BUT I'M BORED!

Being a good parent is not about filling our children's every waking moment. It isn't about stepping in and doing children's imaginative work for them or telling them how to do their play "better" or reaching for another toy when they seem fatigued with the one they have. So don't let that whiny "I'm bored!"

guilt you into action (or into handing over the iPad). Children are driven to play—it is the motor behind their development. And that makes them very boredom averse. Their brains constantly want new things to feed on and test out. But if you always take it on yourself to feed that play motor, children won't discover nearly as many new ways to play. Boredom is not the opposite of play, it is a necessary part of it. Boredom is good for children—it stimulates curiosity. Boredom is the lull before the bright spark of imagination.

"If we always take away their boredom, children's play diet is significantly impoverished."

Learning to be imaginative expands children's horizons and sets them up brilliantly to face the challenges of life. Imagination is what leads children to interact with their environment in new ways, to invent, test out, create, reorder, and investigate. If adults always step in with activities when children are bored, they don't learn to use their imagination to rise to the challenge of boredom. Imagination is like a muscle—a habit of mind—that children develop through practice and repetition. And if children always reach for a screen as an easy boredom filler, then the spark of imagination is also lost.

If your kids are bored, that's great. Celebrate it. They will have to stretch their brains to meet the challenge. Don't feel obliged to take away their boredom by providing things to do. Say, "That's brilliant! What are you going to do about it?" Then step back and give them time. Let them dwell in their own boredom until something sparks. Play ideas need a bit of space to grow.

If your child really can't think of something to do, set them a challenge ("Why don't you see how many different insects you can count in the garden?"). If they don't like your challenge, say, "Well, that's my idea. If you don't like it, you'll have to come up with your own." It is not your job as a parent to take away your child's boredom, it's your job to stay calm and patient while they find their own solution and not let them badger you into doing that creative brain work for them. Learning to manage themselves and their bored feelings is an essential life skill, so take the long view. Children learn how to solve problems by practicing solving problems—and boredom is a great problem to find creative solutions for!

Making space for playfulness lets the joy back into family life. Sometimes that means parents joining in, and sometimes it means us sitting back and leaving the children to it and just enjoying the moment. One of my most vivid memories from when my children were little was the day I realized that play wasn't an added extra or just another task to juggle—it was the whole point of childhood. I remember the moment like yesterday. It was a sunny

Monday in June on a sandy beach in the south of England. We had the beach to ourselves. My kids had found a huge hole that bigger children must have dug on the weekend, and they were having the time of their lives—jumping into the hole, digging tunnels, running free across the beach, playing chase the waves; an absolutely idyllic childhood moment. And I realized in a rush that in this moment they were completely happy. And everything else about how hard it was being a single working parent, the sleepless nights, the battles over bedtime, the sheer relentlessness of how much there was to do every day just fell away in the realization that all of that was just stuff. This moment of play and joy was the entire point of parenting.

ACTION POINTS

- Try out a new play activity with your child(ren) in which you are an equal play partner—not the expert, the boss, or the teacher.
- Identify new places in your local area where your children can spend time outside connecting with the natural world and where you can either relax while you watch them or join in.

II

CALM HOUSE, HAPPY FAMILY

5

Attention Is Your Superpower

Making space for playfulness, building a good relationship with your child, and making sure you walk in the door ready to parent will all go a long way to creating a family life that meets your children's needs and nurtures your well-being. But we all know that parenting is never just going to be about the good stuff. Children are not born knowing how society expects them to behave—how to be kind, how to manage their reactions, or how to ask nicely when they want something. Mustering the energy to manage wayward children when you've already done a full shift at work is one of the biggest challenges for working parents. Finding positive ways to manage children's more difficult behavior can be the difference between a family life we enjoy coming home to and a home that feels like a battleground.

We all have things we'd like our children to stop doing—whether that's whining, shouting, needling their little brother, ignoring your instructions, or refusing to put on their pajamas. But when all your parenting has to be done in a brief window between home time and bedtime, it's easy to slip into incessant reruns of the same battles about the same behavior: "He does that, we explain/shout/ban him from the Xbox. He does that again, we up the stakes and ban him from the Xbox even longer, but nothing seems to work." Coming home after a long day at work to spend your precious family time arguing over who hit who first or cajoling a tantruming child into brushing their teeth isn't fun. It's a miserable way to spend your evenings, on tenterhooks waiting for the next battle to begin. Not the happy family life any of us signed up for.

When parents come to me for support, they usually want a simple solution to the question "How can I stop my child doing X?" Unfortunately, children don't come with a remote control or manual. There is no magic code word to make them change their behavior. Children are works in progress and being childish comes with the territory! As parents, the only thing that we can really control is our own behavior. If we want to change a child's behavior, we first need to change our own. And, crucially, we have to change the way we pay attention.

I know it doesn't always feel like it, but you are the world, the universe, and everything in it to your children. You are their superhero. Your attention is everything to them—it is the magic beam that lights up their lives, that makes them feel alive and connected. Your children crave your attention, not because they are little prima donnas but because they are driven to seek it out: it is essential for their development. Attention is your parental superpower.

Whenever I talk about attention, lots of working parents go straight to "can't": "But I can't give them my attention, I'm not there!" And then from "can't" to guilt and self-blame: "I can't ever give them enough attention because I work and when I am there, I'm exhausted." Children's need for attention is yet another stick to beat ourselves with. But this isn't about "enough" attention, this is about where we direct our attention within the time we have available. When we step away from the guilt and allow ourselves to appreciate how much our attention means to our children, we can learn to deploy it a bit more smartly. For working parents, harnessing the power of your attention is all about focus and intensity, not about quantity. It's not about finding extra hours (or minutes), it's about targeting your attention intelligently in order to create a happy family dynamic and encourage the behavior you want to see.

In most parenting situations, we have choices. That choice often boils down to being either a policeman or a coach. A policeman catches kids getting things wrong and tells them off. A coach teaches children the skills to get it right. For me, positive parenting is all about spending as much time as possible wearing your coach's hat. That means catching children being good and encouraging them to do it more often. And for that, attention is the most powerful tool in your parenting toolbox.

WHY KIDS CRAVE ATTENTION

Often we talk about children's attention seeking in a pejorative way, as an undesirable characteristic ("He's showing off to get attention") or we seize on our child's attention seeking as a guilt stick to whip ourselves with ("She's behaving like that to get my attention because I work and she never gets enough of me"), as if attention seeking is somehow a bad thing. But children's desire for their parents' attention is completely natural and legitimate. Ask any stay-at-home parent; their children seek attention too!

Babies come out of the womb optimized to create connections with the adults around them; they are highly effective attachment-seeking missiles. They achieve this by arousing adults' senses and capturing our attention—by smelling amazing and having big eyes and soft skin. And if that fails, by emitting an ear-piercing noise. Persuading adults to meet their needs is essential to babies' survival. Newborns are so utterly helpless and underdeveloped that if adults were not prepared to enslave themselves to their needs, they would perish. They need the adults looking after them to be so stimulated that they are willing (even in the depths of utter exhaustion) to drag themselves out of bed and prioritize their child's need for food above their own need for sleep. In the early years, lack of a caregiver's attention is life threatening. Successfully securing parental attention is critical, and young children are programmed to do just that.

Adult attention not only keeps children safe and fed, it also has a direct impact on how children's brains get wired up and how they understand their environment. Warm, attentive caregivers help babies to regulate their volatile physical and emotional states. By responding to their cries and soothing them, we help babies to regulate their stress hormones, which in turn influences how babies' brains develop and how they go on to manage stressful situations far into the future. Attention via direct eye contact is an especially information-rich source of learning for infants. Adults' facial expressions are the primary source of social referencing whereby children will look to their adult caregiver's face to check if an environment is safe, to understand if a situation is a cause for alarm (or humor), and to learn from the facial reactions caused by their own actions.

Attention is to kids like sunshine is to plants—they will grow in its direction. As babies mature into children, they learn through experience which behaviors keep that parental attention tap turned on. Through trial and error, action and consequence, they learn how to maintain parents' attention by repeating the behavior that most successfully catches it.

So when you walk in the door—either at home or for the childcare pick-up—and your daughter demands attention, she's just doing what comes naturally. She's not passing judgment on the fact that you have been at work all day (or she has been at nursery). She might express that desire for your attention through joy, anger, tears, or clinginess, by acting out or even by feigning ignoring you in order to draw you in, but what she is expressing is a natural craving for your attention. You can choose to interpret her desire for attention as an expression of lack ("She's not getting enough of me") or you can choose to interpret it as an expression of attachment ("She loves me and is attached to me and therefore wants to be connected with me").

The first interpretation sees the child as a glass half-empty: "If I was around more, or worked fewer days, or was a 'better' parent, or less tired, then I could fill up that glass with attention and then she'd be happier and maybe I'd get some time for myself!" The second interpretation is empowering: your attention is the currency of your connection with your child and a stimulant to learning. She will never have enough of it, attention is not quantifiable into an ideal number of minutes. "She loves my attention so much, she will do anything to get it." When you see it that way, then attention stops being a guilt issue and becomes a transformative force that you can use to teach your children the skills they need and to help create a happy family dynamic.

THINKING POINT

How do you feel when you think about your child's need for attention? Does it make you feel guilty, exhausted, inadequate, or overwhelmed? Or loved, special, and important? Do you think of attention in terms of a finite amount of time and energy to be divided up? What would happen if you visualized your attention differently, such as a beam of warm light?

WHAT ARE YOU PAYING MOST ATTENTION TO?

Be honest: take a step back and have a think about what occupies your attention most during family time. For most working parents, there is so much to squeeze into our nonworking hours that our children are in direct competition with a never-ending list of household tasks (which itself is vying with our personal need to collapse on the sofa for postwork recuperation). Children are utterly driven and tooled-up to secure our attention, and they will do almost anything to succeed (especially if you have just sat down for a cup of tea on the sofa!). But exactly how they succeed in winning our attention is crucial because that will set the course for their future behavior.

When you have lots to do or your energy levels are low, children who are being good are easy to ignore. If children are playing quietly or cooperating with requests, busy parents usually seize the opportunity to get on with some-thing (remember that "ignoring good behavior" parenting hole?!). We might be grateful, we might say "thank you," but our response tends to be muted and low key. Being good has a low attention payoff. So children look to secure our attention in other ways.

Sometimes young children demand your attention through their physical presence—by following you around, climbing on you, taking your hand and leading you to where they want you to be, or physically insisting that you notice them and join in their activities through a persistence that's tiring but hard to ignore. It tends to work or, if it doesn't, it at least garners some nega-tive attention.

Children love positive attention, but they will settle for negative attention if that's what's on offer or if that's easier to get. And if you are the child of an overstretched working parent, negative attention is usually pretty easy to get! By refusing to put your shoes on when dad's in a hurry, for example, or pinch-ing your little sister until she squeals, or careering around the house making a loud noise when mom's on the phone to her boss. We can't help but react to these inconveniences. And often our reactions to children's negative behavior are much bigger and more intense than the half-hearted attention children receive for getting it right. We shout, we argue, we go off like a volcano and generally bring the full force of our attention to their offenses: "Have you no idea how important that phone call was?!" It might not be positive, but shouting at children is a high-intensity form of attention. Recriminations are attention. Debating and explaining are forms of attention. Chasing a runaway toddler down the road is attention.

Children want us to notice them at all costs. And if we fall into the habit of noticing what they do wrong more intensely than what they do right, they can fall into the habit of doing the wrong thing more and more often. Chil-dren repeat the behavior that gets your attention. And when their behavior gets even worse? We bring even more attention to it—lecturing, explaining, shouting, threatening dire consequences—accidentally reinforcing their poor choices with more of our precious attention.

"But I am always telling her what a good girl she is and she still misbehaves!" Unfortunately, in the attention stakes, one "Good girl!" is quickly outweighed by an angry tirade about how many times you've already told her to hang her coat up/put her yogurt cup in the garbage/come to the table/be nice to her sister. If you don't believe me, try keeping an attention diary. Choose a typical week and every evening make a note of each time you give your child atten-tion. Record both the duration of the attention and the intensity. So a snuggly cuddle with some warm comments might be thirty seconds at intensity 4 (on a 1 to 5 scale in which 5 is the highest), whereas a fight over coming off the iPad might be two minutes at intensity 5. You can also note whether the attention was positive or negative and what you were doing before it happened. See what patterns you can find around which behavior your child is using to capture your most intense attention.

POSITIVE PARENTING MAKES YOU HAPPIER

For working parents, time is a precious resource. How much time you spend paying attention to negative behavior matters not only because it sets the course for children's future behavior but also because it directly impacts our happiness levels. Paying too much attention to children's negative behavior colors how we see our children and how we see ourselves. When we focus too much on children's difficult behavior, it's easy to become less satisfied—with our children, with ourselves, and with our lives in general. A negative mood activates our battle stations. When we see our children doing that thing wrong *again* that we have told them about *so* many times, we feel disrespected, not listened to, and trespassed against, and all our antagonistic feelings are triggered. We quickly lose perspective and drift into globalized conclusions. A child who lashes out when angry becomes "He is always angry, he's so difficult." Our own struggles to find a way to help become "I'm such an incompetent parent, I can't cope with him." And too many evenings where it all goes pear-shaped become "Every evening is a nightmare, I dread going home."

On the flipside, focusing on what children are doing well is truly powerful. It profoundly affects the way we think and feel about our children. The more we look for what our children are doing right, the more we see it. The more we notice them getting things right, the more positive we feel about our children, and the more we feel like we might be OK parents after all. Focusing on the good behavior also helps our children to feel positive about themselves. Kids feel great about themselves when we notice them getting it right. And that changes their behavior. The more we notice them getting it right, the more often they will get it right. It's a win–win feel-good spiral. Our perspective becomes a little rosier and we become more content, more satisfied, and happier with our children, ourselves, and our family lives. Our perspective shifts and so does our mood. We become more able to be playful and to tune in to our children and engage more often in those nicer bits of being a parent.

If you have found yourself in a bit of a negative rut, overwhelmed by difficult behavior, or maybe you've just had a bad evening, try a quick gratitude exercise. Sit down for five minutes and think very specifically about the good things your child has done that day/week. Think about their most lovable traits and habits. Feeling grateful and listing the positives has been shown to improve both short- and long-term happiness. And that's got to be worth five minutes of your time! You can even incorporate this into a daily routine with your child—taking a few moments at dinner or bedtime to each think about the best bits of your day, the things that made you happy, in order to shift everyone toward a more optimistic mindset.

One of the best pieces of feedback I've ever had from a parent was after a session discussing the importance of noticing children being good. "It was like someone swapped my children for nicer ones," this parent wrote. "Amazing what a difference a shift in my attitude made. My two were fighting all day and I was shouting all day, now they play nicely *most* of the time and I am a calm parent *most* of the time! It was a revelation."

I can't promise that focusing on what your children are doing right will have quite such a transformative effect in your house, but it will certainly make a difference. Focusing on the positives puts parents in a positive frame of mind, improves our mindset, and helps take the battling out of parenting. And that's a real win for energy-depleted working parents.

> **"Focusing on the positives signposts the route for children to change their behavior."**

HOW DO I STOP HIM DOING X?

"So how am I supposed to stop him doing something if I mustn't pay attention to it?" Well, to wield your parental superpower, you need to target your attention precisely. If you want to change an aspect of your child's behavior, you need to put your coach's hat on and focus on how you *do* want them to behave instead. The trick is to catch your child doing the right thing as often as possible and use your full-beam mommy/daddy attention to encourage them to do it more often.

Step 1: Focus on the behavior you *do* want to see, not the behavior you want to stop.

If there is something you want your child to stop doing, turn it around and think about how you want them to behave instead. What would "good" look like? If the problem is tantrums when you turn off the computer, what would the right behavior be? Turning it off by themselves? Silently skipping off to play with a different toy? Asking politely if they can finish this game before it's turned off? You need to be really clear about exactly what behavior you do want to see because, if you haven't gotten an answer to that question, how is your child supposed to learn how to do it? Behavior doesn't turn off like a tap, we need to replace it with a positive alternative.

Step 2: Double-check that your expectations are reasonable.

A two-year-old is going to struggle to stop playing with something they are enjoying, and they won't be able to use words to tell you about that. A seven-year-old should be able to use words (not fists) to explain their feelings, but they won't be able to stay calm when frustrated. A nine-year-old should be able to keep an eye on the time and be aware of how long they have left on an activity, but that doesn't mean they will want to stop. Aim for a behavior that is an achievable improvement on where your child currently is, not for perfection.

Step 3: Realize that the problem behavior doesn't happen all the time.

Maybe your child sometimes lets you turn off the computer without a fight. Or maybe they usually comply when you turn off the TV (but not the computer). Look for examples of when they get it right and ask yourself how you respond when that happens. Chances are your reactions are a lot more muted than when they get it wrong. How could you deploy your attention more intensely to those "good" moments?

Step 4: Set your attention to full beam.

Changing children's behavior is all about identifying exactly what behavior you want to see and deploying your attention intensely and precisely to encourage more of it. Even if the desirable behavior only happens very occasionally, or only in a different context, focus in on it with your full-beam attention. Next time your son stops any activity and trots off happily when told, with no debate, make a point of saying, "Thank you for listening to me and finishing the game when I asked you. That was brilliant, well done!" Give him a high five, a pat on the back, or a warm smile so he knows that he did the right thing and gets a nice glow inside. Make sure you describe what he has done that you liked so that there is no ambiguity about why he is being praised. Keep switching your attention beam on full power every time he finishes an activity when asked and he'll be motivated to do it more often and in more contexts. The one time he stays calm when you ask him to turn off the computer, even if he is scowling, praise him warmly for doing the right thing. Drop a kiss on his forehead (if he'll let you!) and make him feel proud of getting it right.

There are only so many hours in the day (for children as well as adults!). If we can encourage children to do the right thing a little more often, then there is less time available for them to be doing the wrong thing. If you pay high-quality attention to the behavior that you want your children to repeat—and tell them how much you like it—they will tend to do more of it. The scales will tip a little and, if they are doing a little more of the right behavior, then the wrong behavior inevitably decreases a little too. Your evenings will become a bit calmer, a little snugglier, and a tad less of a battle. And hey presto, you are heading in the right direction for a happier family life.

"But why should I praise him for something he ought to do anyway?" Well, is he already doing it? No. Do you want him to do it? Yes. Are you parenting a hypothetical child or your real child? Standing on that kind of parenting principle is like giving a Level 8 reading book to a child just because that's their educational target even though they can only read at Level 4. It's not going to improve their reading and will result in a very negative interaction. And anyway, don't *you* like a bit of recognition when you are making progress learning to do something you couldn't do before? Think of something you learned to do as an adult that other people learned as a child or teenager—like learning to swim, drive, cook, or put up a shelf—or something you have recently learned to do at work. I bet that someone noticing your progress felt really good. And I bet you felt proud of yourself each time you mastered a new element despite the fact that you were a bit late to the party. Maybe even more so because you were late to pick it up. Perhaps for you there was a bit of an obstacle to overcome, like a fear of water or anxiety about giving presentations. Having someone encouraging you without judging is a big help. Children don't develop in nice straight lines that conform to aggregated averages. If your child isn't doing something (yet), that means they need to learn to do it. And your attention sunbeam will help them learn.

"Focusing your attention on the behavior you do want from your children is a win–win, and those are precious in parenting."

"Won't all that fuss just turn her into a praise junkie who won't do anything without expecting reward?" The key is to use praise as a short-term targeted approach to encourage new behavior rather than a scattergun strategy. Use descriptive praise to tell children exactly what they have done right. For example, "Good girl for taking turns" or "Well done for listening to me and doing what I asked the first time, that was brilliant." Be warm, sincere, and enthusiastic. The aim is for children to feel proud of themselves so that they are self-motivated to get it right again. Praise their effort and progress, even if they don't get it 100 percent right. And once they have bedded in that new habit, you can reduce the praise for that behavior to just occasional nuggets and start working on a different issue instead.

The more time you spend in a win–win dynamic, the happier and more harmonious your family life will be. Catching kids being good makes you feel more positive and it makes your children feel more positive. They get your attention and you get your desired result of a bit more of the right behavior more often. Of course, children won't get it right every time—getting it wrong is part of the journey and how children learn. There will still be times when you need to respond to unacceptable behavior. And if your child is being aggressive or is in danger of hurting themselves, you will need to find a way to manage that behavior actively (but preferably without shouting). Which leads us neatly on to the next chapter!

ACTION POINTS

- Keep an attention diary—for an evening, a weekend, or a whole week. Make a note every time you give your child intense and focused attention (either positive or negative). Record the duration and intensity of the attention and what triggered it. What patterns do you find?
- Make a list of three things you want your child(ren) to stop doing. What behavior do you want them to do in those moments instead? Make a conscious effort to look out for that desirable behavior (in any context) and praise them whenever you see it.
- Spend a few minutes each day being grateful about your child. You can do this alone by focusing on the positive or exceptionally lovable things your child has done that day/week or as part of a daily ritual talking about the best bits of your day with your child.

6

How Not to Shout

No parent has endless patience. Personally, my patience has strengthened a little through raising children, but when they are giving out the medals at the Patient Parenting Olympics, you will find me applauding in the stands, not on the podium. For a long time, I believed that this lack of patience was stopping me from being the nonshouty parent I wanted to be. At the end of my rope, after yelling like a fishwife yet again, I would beat myself up for failing to stay calm and promise that next time I would do better. But next time, exactly the same thing would happen:

Me: Please tidy your room.

Son: (*Ignores me.*)

Me: Please go and tidy your room.

Son: (*Pretends he didn't hear.*)

Me: (*A little louder.*) I said go and tidy your room. Don't ignore me, that's really rude.

Son: It doesn't need tidying. It's fine.

Me: (*Getting wound up now.*) It does need tidying . . . (*Long list of reasons why it does need tidying.*)

Son: Stop stressing. I'll do it later.

Me: (*Well and truly wound up now, high volume.*) If you don't go and tidy your room right NOW, I will do X. (*Followed by a tirade of ridiculous threats and emotional messages.*)

Not pretty. My postargument analysis would oscillate between blaming my son and, once I'd calmed down, blaming myself for not having the infinite patience that was clearly required for nonshouty parenting.

We all know in theory that shouting at our children isn't a great idea. None of us embarked on parenting with "Shouty Mom/Dad" as our ideal destination. But somewhere along the way we get sucked into it, especially when nothing else seems to work and the kids just won't do as they're told. Most working parents shout because we've run out of options or energy, or both. Then we feel terrible. Because we feel like failures. Because we want our families to be happy places. Because we believe we should be more patient, more creative, or just better at parenting in some unfathomable way that we can't quite figure out. Or we blame our children for making us shout.

But having limited patience doesn't make you a terrible parent, it just means you are a human being. We all have limited patience. There are some amazingly laidback people in the world who don't ever seem to get riled by anything, but even they have their breaking points (and sometimes all the more shocking because they are unexpected). Switching from work mode to parent mode does not mean finding a saintly level of patience and never hurrying our children to do anything. That's ridiculous. The secret of nonshouty parenting isn't patience, it's recognizing your own trigger points and stepping in early to prevent your shout buttons getting pushed too often.

"If you really want to be a nonshouty parent, you need to recognize and manage your human limitations rather than aspiring to impossible ideals."

The first step on that journey is self-awareness. If I ask my children to do something important (or to stop doing something that really does need to stop) and they don't cooperate, I now know myself well enough to predict that if I keep asking and asking or if I engage in debate or reasoning or if I resort to pleading or threatening and asking again, my big red "disrespect alarm" will go off. My emotions will shoot sky high and I will end up shouting. That's me, I'm human. So if I don't want that to happen, I need to get off that path a little earlier and act while I am still calm rather than waiting until I have already lost it. If I want my children to do something that's really important, I state clearly what I want to happen and, if it isn't complied with, I don't engage in debate, I don't shout, I don't threaten ("If you don't do X then Y will happen"), I don't cajole, I just give the instruction twice and then follow through.

Inevitably, that doesn't always make my kids happy. Maybe you are judging me harshly for it too? (Or maybe that's just the always-critical voice in my head.) Because parenting calmly and consistently on the outside can mean managing some difficult feelings on the inside, especially as a working parent. Saying "No" to children and backing up our rules with consequences can make us unpopular with precisely the little people we love and care about most in the world—the very people on whose behalf we are expending all this energy and putting ourselves on the line daily in that grueling commute and exhausting juggling act. Backing up boundaries can mean shouldering some intense negative feedback from our kids about how badly we are doing at the very thing that matters most to us in the whole world—bringing them up. While all the time never really being sure whether we are doing the right thing anyway.

But we have to do it. Because children need boundaries. They need to know where the lines are that mustn't be crossed—like hitting their brother, running into the road, or leaving garbage on the floor for someone else to pick up. They need to learn what behavior is and isn't acceptable so they can get along with others and get on in life. And it's our job as grown-ups to draw those lines and help them learn.

"Our children need us to stand firm and be in control so they can find their feet on solid ground."

THINKING POINT

Next time you find yourself shouting at your child, spend some time replaying the incident in your head once you have calmed down. Focus on your side of the interaction, not your child's. At what point did your volume start to rise? Can you think of any action you could have taken before your volume started to rise that would have changed the situation?

BALANCING WARMTH AND CONTROL

Research on parenting styles consistently highlights that children benefit from a balanced combination of warmth and control. An assertive parenting style that combines a nurturing and affectionate relationship with firm boundaries and clear expectations is consistently associated with positive outcomes for children—mentally, socially, and academically. It's not rocket science: firm but kind, warm but with clear rules, loving plus consistent expectations. Both sides of that equation are needed. Taking away either pole is linked to poorer outcomes for children (with the absence of both warmth and control being the most harmful).

Most of us naturally err toward one pole or the other on the warmth/control balancing act. Within reason, that's OK, but the aim is to combine warmth and control in a thoughtful balance. And for working parents especially, that can be a challenge. When we are running on empty at the end of the day and the kids won't cooperate, it's easy to default to our preferred style, clicking into discipline mode or resorting to coaxing or giving in or veering from one to the other, tearing ourselves apart trying to work out which response we should be using in this particular situation. And if we already feel guilty about how little time we have with our children, that can compound our uncomfortable feelings about disappointing them by saying "No." We love our kids to pieces, and it's hard to see them disappointed, frustrated, or angry, especially when we are the source of that discomfort.

But enforcing essential boundaries—especially around the way people treat each other—is absolutely crucial for children's development. Clear, consistent boundaries help children to develop good social skills and learn to express themselves in ways that respect the needs of others. Children need to learn to follow instructions and adhere to simple rules if they are to make positive choices. These are skills that will help them get on better at school and in life in general. Not to mention that children who cooperate are a lot easier to get along with in your own family!

Some parents hope that a laissez-faire approach will allow children to grow and blossom in their own unique ways. But backing up boundaries is not the same as trying to turn children into robots. Clear boundaries actually give children a much greater chance of realizing their potential because they help children to develop self-control. And self-control is exactly what makes it more likely that children will flourish and fulfill their own unique potential. Learning to control your impulses and sacrifice immediate pleasures for a longer-term gain is the basis of all self-discipline, and it is through self-discipline that children's innate talents become actual expertise. Your son may have the inherent potential to be a concert pianist, but without the self-discipline to put in the hours of practice, he will never be one. In fact, self-control has been shown to be a better predictor of success for a child than any other factor, including IQ.

Children need adults to set limits and provide learning through clear explanations and consistent boundaries, exactly the same as they need us to feed them, keep them warm, play with them, cuddle them, and talk with them. Learning how to set those limits without shouting will make your family a much more enjoyable place to be and somewhere you look forward to coming home to.

THE SECRET OF CALM PARENTING

Being a nonshouty parent isn't about patience. It's about having a reasonable plan and sticking to it as much as you possibly can. Calm parenting is really about managing yourself and your own actions, not your children, and being proactive rather than reactive. And if you can do that, you will have a house in which shouting is the exception not the rule.

Usually, shouting starts off as a last resort—we ask calmly, we ask calmly, we ask calmly, and when we still get ignored after all that asking calmly, we end up shouting. But shouting quickly becomes a habitual dynamic. The children learn that mom/dad doesn't really mean what they say until they start shouting. And mom/dad learns that they might as well just go straight to shouting because that's the only thing that ever works. We learn that to get our children to listen, we need to shout, and children learn to ignore mom/dad until they are shouting. And so all the small things quickly escalate into shouting.

What's the solution? First, never start an interaction by shouting. Parents often shout simply because we are in a different room. This is a classic hectic working parent trap! We are always in a hurry, so we save time by shouting up the stairs to the kids rather than walking up to speak to them. Or we holler from the kitchen to the living room to tell them that dinner is ready. But if you yell instructions to your children from a distance, you are asking to be ignored. Especially if you are telling your child to stop doing something they like (for example, watching TV) or to do something they are not so keen on (for example, brushing their teeth). They will just pretend they didn't hear you.

And what happens when the kids ignore you? You shout louder. Or more fiercely. Your emotions start to rise. Because if you've started an interaction with your voice raised, you are already halfway to losing your cool. It might all start off calmly, but after you have shouted that instruction louder and louder several times, you will definitely start to feel annoyed: "This kid is wasting my time, doesn't he know how busy I am? The last thing I want to do after a hard day at work is come home and cook but I've done it and there's a lovely meal on the table and he's just completely ignoring me. He's so ungrateful and disrespectful!" And once you are shouting *and* annoyed, things will only go downhill. Our minds and bodies are very closely linked: if we raise our voices, our emotions will soon follow.

Instead, if you need to speak to your child, either to give an instruction or in response to poor behavior, get up close. Yes, I know you're busy. But believing those few seconds are worth saving by shouting from a distance is a classic efficiency thinking trap. Those few seconds of time are not worth the negative impacts of an interaction full of anger, and once you've been ignored twice, that tiny time saving will be lost anyway. So walk up those stairs, into the living room, or down to the end of the garden and go up to your child. Bend down to their eye level (if they are little) and speak in a calm voice. We instinctively don't shout in people's faces, so if you are up close—about an arm's length away—and addressing your child face to face, your voice is likely to drop in volume automatically. (And if you're in a state where you might shout in your child's face, you definitely need to remove yourself and find somewhere to calm down.)

Your child is much more likely to cooperate if you get close to them. You are just a lot harder to ignore up close! And even if they don't cooperate, you are at least ready to deal with that noncooperation calmly and with a clear head. Because when our volume stays down, our emotions and stress levels stay down too.

HOW TO TALK SO CHILDREN WILL
DO WHAT THEY'RE ASKED

How and when we give instructions also has a huge impact on the chances of children complying with them. Young children have such a strong inner urge to play that asking them to stop playing and come and do something less interesting instead is always going to leave the odds stacked against you. So if you can, try to time your requests so that they coincide with a lull in play or the end of a game. Just because you have walked into the house with a long postwork to-do list does not mean that right now is the best moment to tell your daughter to go tidy her room! Signal in advance that there is only a short time left for playing so that your child gets used to the idea. For example, give a five-minute warning that after this game, it's tidy up time. It won't work every time, but it does increase the chances of cooperation, especially if you can present the new activity as something potentially fun or likely to include some of that lovely mommy/daddy attention.

Keep your instructions simple. All parents think our children are incredibly bright. Of course we do, we love them and see the best in them. But sometimes we talk to children using a lot of nuance ("Well, isn't that nice, having to tidy up a messy house after a long day at work!"). Or we don't really explain exactly what we want them to do ("Sam, stop being silly"). Or we explain far too much all at once ("You mustn't jump on the sofa because sofas are really expensive and I can't afford to replace it because I'm still paying off the car and I'm saving for our vacation"). Young children's working memories are still developing—the more words we add into our request, the more likely they are to miss what the request was in the first place. And their understanding of "not being silly" is probably very different from ours!

If you really want your child to do something, give a precise, simple instruction in a calm voice that tells them exactly what they should do: "*Please do this.*" Very simple, very clear, very calm. If you want them to stop doing something, tell them what to do instead: "*Please stop jumping on the sofa, put your bottom on the sofa*" or "*Please stop jumping on the sofa, jump on the floor instead.*"

Be careful about muddling up explanations and instructions. Modern parents love to explain things to our children, to tell them why they must/mustn't do something. And it's really important for children's learning that we do this. After all, we want them to comply because they understand the reasons, not out of sheer obedience. But sometimes, with young children, too many explanatory words can get in the way, and the instruction gets lost in the middle. And for older children, explanations can be seized upon to debate the instruction and avoid complying with the request ("But you can just get a different job that pays more money and then we can buy a new sofa." *Bounce, bounce!*). Once children have engaged you in a debate about your explanations, bingo! They've secured your attention and delayed cooperating.

Remember to get up close to your child when you give an instruction and only repeat the instruction twice. That's right. Only repeat the instruction twice. If you've gotten up close and you know your daughter can hear you and she doesn't cooperate after a second request, then take it as read that she has decided to ignore you. Asking again will not increase the chances of cooperation. But it will result in you getting frustrated and ending up angry, shouting, or losing your Zen because you are not being listened to. And don't resort to threatening. Counting to three or saying what will happen if they don't cooperate just teaches children to wait until you start counting to three or threatening consequences before they cooperate. If you consistently follow through after two requests, children will quickly learn to cooperate when they are asked and not wait until you get to "two-and-three-quarters" or start shouting threats about dire consequences.

Give a simple instruction, then wait. If your child does what you ask, acknowledge their cooperation. Praise them. Say "thank you." Turn your attention superpower to full beam to make them want to cooperate every time you ask! Don't be tempted into a lecture about why they should have got it right the first time without being told—just positively reinforce their cooperation with a warm smile and a pat on the back. If you need to explain, now is a good time: "*Thank you for listening. I know you were enjoying bouncing but the springs in the sofa will get broken if you jump on it and then we won't be comfortable when we snuggle up to watch the TV.*" If your child doesn't cooperate, ask a second time to give them one more chance. And if that still doesn't work, be proactive and follow through with a suitable brief consequence before anyone has a chance to get wound up.

NINE GOLDEN RULES FOR USING CONSEQUENCES

One of the primary ways that young children learn is through cause and effect. "*I do X, and Y happens; I like Y so I will do X again. I do W, and Z happens; I don't like Z therefore I won't do W again.*" Providing simple, direct consequences is an effective tool for structuring children's choices in order to encourage cooperation and discourage unacceptable behavior. Structuring children's choices through consequences means that next time they are more likely to choose the right path.

Consequences work best when you follow these nine golden rules.

1. Consequences should be nonhurtful.

The purpose of a consequence is not to punish a child or to make them feel bad. The purpose of a consequence is to provide an outcome that has fewer payoffs than if your child had chosen a better course of action. A consequence should always be implemented in a way that clearly identifies the behavior that is unwanted rather than labeling the child as bad or inherently naughty.

2. Consequences should always be delivered calmly.

If you have got yourself worked up, then you have probably left it too late and you needed to step in earlier. A straightforward calm sentence is all that is required: *"I asked you to stop throwing the toy at your sister because it is dangerous and you didn't. I'm going to take away the toy for two minutes."*

3. Consequences should be predictable.

The purpose of a consequence is to provide a clear distinction between making a good choice and making a poor choice. Therefore a good consequence is one that a child can reasonably predict will happen if they choose a particular course of action. Children can predict what is right and wrong when they have clear rules (or are given a clear instruction) and when consequences are applied in a consistent way.

Parents often think that it is the severity of a consequence that makes a difference, but it isn't. It's the consistency. If the same consequence happens every single time, then a child will learn much more quickly to change their behavior. They can predict what the result of their actions will be and therefore make a different choice. If when your child refuses to help with cleaning up time, you sometimes follow through with a consequence and sometimes just do it for them, they won't learn from that so well and are more likely to keep refusing to help.

4. Consequences should be immediate.

The best consequences happen immediately so that the link between the behavior and the consequence is crystal clear. Delaying consequences for misbehavior can really dilute their effectiveness for younger children as they may not see the connection. Consequences work from about two and a half years of age—any younger than that and children don't have the cognitive or language skills to understand them or to make choices to avoid them.

As children get older, they can cope with delayed consequences a bit better. So for a nine-year-old, cheating on screen time limits on Wednesday might mean reduced tech time on Thursday. But be careful about delaying consequences too much as they can land you in a parenting quagmire. What if your child is as good as gold before you implement the consequence? Are you going to change your mind? Or stick to your guns and feel mean?

5. Consequences should be brief.

Our win as a parent is always that children do the right thing. So keep consequences short and give your child a second chance as soon as possible. Taking a toy away for a couple of minutes is plenty of time for a young child, no longer than five to ten minutes for an older child. If they still make the wrong choice when given a second chance, you can impose the consequence again for a slightly longer period. But don't reach for big numbers like a whole week. How are they going to learn to get it right if they don't get the chance to practice? And how conflicted are you going to feel after four days when they are being angelic and want their favorite toy back? The aim is to have a few minutes of an undesirable outcome, not a whole week of recriminations.

6. The best consequences are logical.

Try to choose a consequence that logically fits the situation. If your child is throwing a toy, take away the toy. If your children are arguing over the remote control, turn off the TV. If your child is playing dangerously on the swing, remove them from the swing. Logical consequences help children see the connection between cause and effect. Consequences could also include getting your child to clear up a mess they have made or to take the natural consequences for something that they have made happen (like not being able to use something because they have broken it).

7. Consequences should remove positive payoffs.

Because play and attention are such key drivers for children, the best consequences remove play and attention for a few minutes. They take play away from the child (for example, removing a toy or activity) or they take the child away from play.

8. Don't make a drama out of it.

Consequences should always be low attention and low drama. So step in early and implement a brief, logical consequence before you get wound up. Explain calmly what is happening and why. Ignore any fuss or complaints and don't get into a debate. The best consequences make children a bit bored and take the focus off them.

9. Positive consequences for getting it right.

Consequences work best when there is a clear difference in outcomes between doing the right thing and doing the wrong thing. Doing the wrong thing results in a brief consequence, which is dull, boring, or just not particularly desirable, whereas doing the right thing results in lots of lovely reinforcing positive attention from mom and dad. If a particular behavior is really entrenched and you find yourself in an escalating battle, applying ever-greater consequences for the same behavior again and again then switching to a motivation strategy and introducing a reward system for the right behavior might be a better way to go. If you are going to use rewards, just make sure you define clearly and specifically what good looks like and focus on one thing at a time. A single issue reward chart for "Being gentle with your sister" (that is, not hitting or kicking her) or "Using kind words with your brother" (that is, not being nasty or winding him up) will help focus children's minds on exactly which behavior they need to do more of. Vague reward charts for "Being good" will probably end up in an argument with your child about what constitutes good and whether a reward should be given!

THINKING POINT

Is there a specific behavior that your child does that particularly winds you up and pushes your shout buttons? What could you do to motivate your child to choose an alternative behavior more often?

SHOULD I USE TIME OUT?

Lots of parents have mixed feelings about removal strategies like Time Out. Some parents find them invaluable, while other parents can't get them to work or choose not to use them. Used well, removal strategies can calm things down and draw a line if a situation is escalating or if there is aggressive behavior. They give both children and parents a chance to calm down and reflect. And they send a powerful message that certain behaviors are unacceptable.

Removal strategies work on exactly the same principle as other conse-quences and the same golden rules apply—you calmly remove the positive payoffs of play and attention but by removing the child not the activity. The lowest level of removal strategy involves removing a child from an activity but keeping them in the same room or immediate vicinity. You just ask them to sit down on the edge of the activity for a couple of minutes. They can't join in the play and they don't get any attention while sitting there. This type of "Sit It Out" removal strategy can be a good option for younger children. It's also a completely portable strategy, so it's great if you are out and about. I know parents who successfully use a few minutes of Sit It Out time at play groups, at the park, or at the supermarket (but I definitely recommend that you get it working at home before you try using it in front of people!).

The ultimate removal strategy is Time Out (often called the Naughty Step). This involves removing a child to another room or to a safe and boring space where they must sit quietly for a few minutes. The parent explains why the child is being removed (a single sentence, not a lecture!), and the child is required to sit quietly for a few minutes. The time doesn't start until the child is sitting quietly. If the child gets up off the Time Out spot, they are calmly returned to it and the time restarts until they have sat quietly for the full required time.

Time Out has had some bad press in recent years, with claims that it involves rejecting your child or trampling on their emotions. Intuitively, when we're faced with a woeful preschooler who doesn't want to sit on that step, that explanation can chime with our parental fears and feelings. There are some children for whom Time Out is not appropriate, such as a child who has experienced trauma or who has separation/attachment issues. And there are definitely situations when Time Out is not appropriate, such as when a child is anxious or distressed. But otherwise, the research data on Time Out is consistent—when implemented calmly in the context of a loving and positive relationship as a strategy of last resort (for example, for aggressive behavior), it is an effective and nonharmful way to help children learn appropriate behavior and regulate their own emotions. Indeed, a consistent consequence routine that combines positive reinforcement for the right behavior plus age-appropriate explanations and Time Outs for major misdemeanors has consistently been shown to increase prosocial behavior and reduce unwanted behaviors. The data is consistent to the point of being boring, which might be why alternative viewpoints have gained traction!

Claims that removal strategies emotionally harm children or damage parent–child relationships play into many working parents' fears about spending time away from our children. Being a working parent already means managing difficult emotions like guilt and worrying that our separation is somehow not good for our children. Much of the research that has been used to argue against Time Out is based on extreme scenarios that involve emotional neglect or harsh parenting rather than a loving family home in which a child is occasionally asked to sit in a certain safe spot in response to whacking their sister over the head with a saucepan.

Certainly, you shouldn't be reaching for Time Out as a first option, so don't overdo it and slip into "policeman" parenting. Time Out works best when it is reserved for serious or aggressive behavior, and it should always be contrasted with lots of positive attention for the right behavior. A happy family dynamic involves imposing consequences when needed but aiming to spend as much time as possible using reinforcing strategies such as praise and attention to encourage the right behavior. Kind but firm. Warm with clear boundaries. Loving plus clear expectations appropriately backed up. Sounds easy, doesn't it?!

And whatever you do, under no circumstances reach for Time Out in the mornings when you are rushing to get to work and have a deadline to get out of the house. For that particular scenario, you are going to need a whole different set of tools for your toolbox!

ACTION POINTS

- Every time you tell your child to "stop" doing something, tell them what to "start" doing instead. Praise them when they cooperate.
- If you need to give your child an instruction, time it well, get up close, give a simple instruction, and only ask twice.

7

Stress-Free Mornings

Switching between work mode and parent mode is all about standing down your time-focused efficiency thinking and understanding that your child's mind is governed by different drivers. That can be a real challenge when you absolutely do need to get out of the house on time! The big problem with mornings is that there genuinely is no time to slow down and chase that shiny wrapper or interrogate the whys and wherefores of how the moon stays in the sky. Children's and parents' needs are in direct conflict in the mornings, and the results are not always pretty.

For most working parents, our mornings are timed to the minute. When my children were little, they needed to be fed, dressed, and out of the house by 7:45 a.m. so that I could get them to nursery by 8:00 a.m. I had to be at work by 8:45 a.m. on the dot so that I could fit in a full day before picking up the children again before nursery closed at 5:30 p.m. Every morning, I'd join a little band of parents standing outside the nursery door at one minute before opening time, waiting to drop our children off at the earliest possible moment.

Some mornings were OK, some were a bit cranky, but mostly they were terrible. The kids woke up ridiculously early and, after they had sprayed breakfast cereal around the kitchen, I would turn on the TV and let them play while I showered and got dressed. But no matter how early we started the process, dragging them back upstairs and getting them dressed always took much longer than it needed to. I would get more and more stressed at the ticking away of time until a missing sock or lost shoe sent me screeching over the precipice. The fifteen-minute car journey to nursery would be filled with me haranguing my children for making us late, again, or for being utterly incapable of think-ing about anyone else other than themselves. A truly miserable start to the day.

Sound familiar? Mornings can be horrible when you are a working parent with young children. There is so much to do in such a short space of time—dressing, breakfast, dishes, tooth brushing, bag packing, shoes, coats—and if your children are little (or just wanting to chase that shiny wrapper) then each one of those tasks can involve huge amounts of parental input. Timekeeping in the morning is just not flexible—the deadlines are absolute. We have to be at certain places at certain times. Your train isn't going to wait because your toddler had a tantrum about his shoes, and you can't expect your boss to be understanding just because your tween couldn't find her geography project again. There's really important stuff at stake here—our professional reputa-tion, our income. Being on time for work matters. We don't want to appear unreliable or flaky or to jeopardize our career progression (or our jobs). Com-bining important deadlines with children whose brains are not yet primed to focus on a task is bound to be stressful.

Lots of the working parents I know resort to ultra-efficiency mode in the mornings and adopt the Sergeant Major approach: "Get out of bed! Put your pants on! Do this now! Do this now!" We push, drag, or bully our children through their morning tasks, prompting and nagging them at every stage to do the things we want them to do. And it can work, for a while. But the Sergeant Major approach is not a lot of fun to be on the other end of and it can also take a nasty turn when we end up shouting. Because when children feel pushed and hurried, they often resort to sabotaging the morning routine through uncooperative behavior or noncompliance—through tantrums, "go-slow," mode, and ignoring instructions. Or just running away with their socks.

And what do you do then? Discipline strategies don't work well in the mornings. Any response that involves time is absolutely useless in the morn-ings. Strategies like Time Out or the Naughty Step all add to morning stress because they risk making us even later. The point of a working parent's morn-ing is to go quickly, not slowly!

Mornings are the ideal conditions for making poor parenting decisions. We've got so much to do and everything's a rush, especially if we're tired, the kids got up late, we can't find things, or we didn't have enough time or energy the night before to get organized. We get that feeling of panic rising inside and find ourselves making ridiculous emotional decisions. Like having a go at a two-year-old for deliberately making us late for our meeting. Or hurling emotional grenades to make our seven-year-old feel guilty about behaving like a child(!). And we do the same thing again and again every morning, despite the fact that it isn't working. We stick like glue to our morning routine because we think it ought to work (or maybe it used to work) and then we blame our children and get frustrated when it doesn't work, yet again.

Short of leaving the house before the kids wake up, there isn't a single magic solution that will turn your mornings into an oasis of calm. Everybody's set-up is different, and the best morning routine is the one that works for you. The key to designing a calmer, happier morning routine that really works is to identify what's causing problems and use a bit of positive psychology to do things differently.

WHY CHILDREN DRAG THEIR FEET IN THE MORNINGS

The heat of the moment is never a good time to think. So find yourself a comfy spot and half an hour's peace and take some time to reflect on what's going on in your morning routine. What's happening and why?

The first thing to understand about mornings is that adults and children have completely different priorities. As a working parent, your morning priority is to get everyone out of the house on time, preferably appropriately fed and dressed, with clean teeth and all the equipment needed for the day. You are in your element when it comes to superdeveloped efficiency thinking because getting to the end goal as quickly as possible really is the point in the morning!

But getting out of the house on time is probably not your child's priority. As we've already seen, young children have two major priorities that pretty much trump all other factors: play and attention. Children are compelled to seek out play and attention—to investigate that shiny wrapper (and want to show it to you too) and forget all about their pants. Sustaining focus on a dull task is just not the way they are wired.

You getting to work on time is not your child's priority. You need to accept that. Because no amount of haranguing or emotional blackmail is going to change it. With the best will in the world, your child doesn't really understand what you do all day at work. How could he? The world of work is completely outside his terms of reference. You sit at a computer all day? Sounds brilliant! Nothing stressful about that—best day ever!

Young children aren't capable of standing in an adult's shoes. That's not a moral judgment, it's a matter of brain development. Under the age of four, children lack the cognitive sophistication to see the world from another person's perspective. We know this from false belief experiments. Show a three-year-old a box of sweets and ask them what they think is inside the box and (as long as they recognize the brand) they will logically answer that there are sweets inside. If you have sneakily replaced the sweets and you open up the box to reveal pencils instead, that surprises them. Because they were expecting sweets! But if you then close the box and bring a new child into the room and ask the original child what this new child will think is in the box, a three-year-old will answer "pencils." Because they know there are pencils in the box. They have seen them. And they can't make the imaginative leap to stand in the new child's shoes and imagine that they haven't seen the pencils and that they are only seeing the box from the outside. Three-year-olds don't have a fully developed "theory of mind" that appreciates that other people have different thoughts in their heads than they do.

So expecting a young child to step inside your adult head and understand how much it matters to you to get to work on time is doomed to failure. Young children simply can't understand why you get so stressed about getting to work. Or what you do when you are at work. Or why it all matters. Or even what "time" is. (My three-year-old once told me he would love me "for three weeks." I think he meant "forever" but three weeks was the longest period of time he could think of!) And nor should children understand those things, because they're children.

Even older children will struggle to imagine adult life or understand adult concerns. Beyond knowing that they should be kind and a good friend, feeling responsible for someone else's life and future (in the way that parents are) is completely alien to them. They aren't familiar with making decisions that involve weighing up lots of competing factors from different angles. As far as they are concerned, if your job stresses you out, why don't you just get a different one? If your boss won't give you enough money, get money from somewhere else. Yes, older kids can compare going to work with going to school and needing to be on time for the bell. But for them, school is something they have no choice about. They have to go to school and be on time because adults say so, not because they are internally motivated. School is an externally imposed imperative. Most young children would much rather take the day at their own pace and connect with their friends in other ways than at school. They don't have that boiling sense of pressure inside to get to school that parents have about getting to work. Children can recognize your stress because it impacts them, but they can't really empathize with why you feel it.

You need to accept that your kids have different priorities and different thoughts from you. This is really important. Because if you interpret children's actions according to adult drivers, then the conclusions you reach will fuel negative thoughts and conflict. Take a child who persistently resorts to go-slow mode in the mornings. If you interpret that behavior as coming from someone who understands your desperate need to get out of the house quickly, then it's only a short hop to concluding, "He knows how much this matters to me, he's doing it deliberately to hurt/annoy me." Every time he is slow to respond will fuel that sense of grudge and of being trespassed against. How we interpret children's intentions determines our emotional reaction to their actions. When we feel repeatedly trespassed against, we are far more likely to shift to anger and lose our temper. Inflamed by a sense of being wronged, we get hurled off the cliff of parenting patience by the lightest of triggers.

Children don't sabotage your morning routine (or any other part of your day) in order to make you late. They do it because they are children and have different priorities. Mornings are a classic win–lose situation. If children meet their "win" of getting lots of play and attention, parents will find it very hard to meet their "win" of getting out of the house on time all clean and dressed and without forgetting anything. Bludgeoning your children into caring about being late simply won't work. And mornings full of shouting are a terrible way for both parents and children to start the day. If you want a calmer, happier morning routine, you are going to have to bring your priorities into alignment and find the win–win.

IDENTIFYING YOUR MORNING PITFALLS

If things are going wrong with your morning routine, then this is one of the times when using your wonderful adult analytical front-brain efficiency thinking will really help you to find a solution. So we are going to put our work heads on for a moment and start with some objective analysis. Keeping track through a diary process can be really useful here. When we are stuck in the middle of a problem, it can feel like something always happens—"My child always has a tantrum about their breakfast in the mornings"—when actually it just happens three mornings out of five. Or it can feel like a tantrum lasts a really long time when in reality it's only ten minutes. We get sucked into that "negative thinking" parenting hole, labeling every morning as a disaster and our children as uncooperative, and we revert to "behavior police" mode. We don't see what goes well (or, indeed, why it goes well). Keeping a morning diary is a good way to stand back, gather facts, and test your assumptions.

There are two ways you could do this:

1. through a simple diary, noting down every morning what problem occurred—where, when, how long, what triggered it, and how it was resolved; or
2. using a tally system—How often did that behavior happen this morning?

You'll need to keep it going for a couple of weeks to get an accurate picture. Keeping track can help you to see patterns and links that you weren't aware of. Maybe the tantrums are more common on Monday mornings after the weekend. Or on Wednesdays when you have to get up earlier. Keeping track might reveal these links.

Another useful tool for analysis is to make a task list. Make a list of every single task that has to be completed as part of your morning routine. Be honest. Write down absolutely everything and group the tasks according to who is supposed to be doing them. This list is going to be really handy when it comes to making changes.

TASK LIST

Parent's tasks: Make coffee, heat milk, take milk to child, unload dishwasher, shower, choose clothes, get dressed, choose child's clothes, dress child, brush child's hair, make breakfast, eat breakfast, feed child, make packed lunches, load dishwasher, supervise tooth brushing, pack own bag, pack child's bag, tidy up toys, collect shoes and coats, put child's shoes and coat on, load everyone into car.

Child's tasks: Drink milk, eat breakfast (doesn't do), brush teeth.

Then think about the order in which events are happening. For example, your morning sequence might be: wake up, make breakfast (for me and kids), shower, get dressed, make packed lunches, get bags ready, get everyone into their coats and shoes. And for your child? Wake up, have breakfast, play, get dressed (after being shouted at), play some more, get manhandled into my shoes and coat.

Identify where in that sequence the problems are occurring and where in that sequence people's priorities are being met. For the parent, most likely, our priority is met at the end of the sequence once everyone is up, fed, dressed, and out of the house. A child's priority, however, is play. So if play is happening in the middle of their sequence, then the child's priority is being met in the middle of their morning routine rather than at the end, which is likely to cause problems. Because if your child has met their priority and is happily playing, why would they want to stop doing that in order to do something they don't want to do (like getting dressed or putting their shoes on)?

"A stress-free morning routine is one that works for everyone and balances everyone's needs."

Another way you can unpick your morning routine is by looking at where things happen. Mapping where problems happen can also help to illuminate why problems might be occurring. Do the problems occur when your child is supposed to be getting dressed? Where are they doing that? Is it in their bedroom? Is there something in their bedroom that is distracting them (for example, toys)? Or are the biggest problems when they have to put their shoes on? Where are their shoes? Somewhere where they can see the TV? A child's inner drive to play can easily override your imperative for them to get ready, so the places in the home where there are obvious play opportunities are often the same places where the morning routine goes off the rails.

Once you have identified the problem areas and obstacles in your particular morning routine, it's time to make changes.

DO LESS IN A DIFFERENT ORDER

The first step in making changes is to reduce your workload. Too much stuff to do in the morning leads to stress. So aim to do less. Look at your morning task list and for every single task ask yourself these four key prioritization questions:

1. Does it have to be done at all?
2. Does it have to be done so well?
3. Can it be done by someone else?
4. Can it be done at a different time?

Be ruthless. Choosing clothes, packing bags, and making sandwiches can all definitely be done the night before. Choose the ingredients carefully and packed lunches can even be batch made once a week and frozen. Could you take a bath the night before instead of a shower in the morning? Can you put the coffee on a timer so it makes itself? Can you leave the dishes and deal with them when you get home? Or move them on to someone else's task list? One parent I know even admitted to putting her toddler to bed in her clothes for the next day when she was really pushed for time!

I'll bet there are things you are doing that could be moved on to your child's task list. For sure, you might need to teach your child to do some new things to make that happen. If your daughter doesn't know how to brush her own hair, then you will need to help her learn. If you want her to make her own breakfast, then the breakfast things are going to have to be kept where she can reach them. You might need to show her how to pour milk or butter toast, or you might need to adapt what she eats so that she can manage it independently.

Don't keep doing things just because you've always done them. Teach your child to be independent and hand over responsibility. And don't underexpect. If your son is expected to clear away his lunch dishes at school, there is no reason why he can't do that at home after breakfast. Being given responsibility prepares children for life and is a real booster for their self-esteem. There might be a time investment in reallocating tasks, but it's not unlike having a new hire at work. It takes a while to show them the ropes, and at first it feels like it would just be quicker to do it yourself. But in the long run, if you show them how to do stuff, it frees you up to do other things.

Be warned, your child may not do things exactly to your standards. The dishes in the dishwasher might be a bit wonky. There might be spills to start with. Their pants drawer will get messed up. But they will get better with practice and they will be learning essential life skills. If you micromanage the mornings and insist on the dishes always being lined up in exactly the right way, you will always be loading the dishwasher yourself. Lowering your standards might be the price to pay for doing less. Having less to do reduces your stress, which will really help to defuse morning conflict.

Once you have reallocated the tasks, reorder the morning sequence to make sure that everyone's priorities are met at the same time at the end of the process. This is your win–win! So for example, if TV is interrupting the routine or causing problems, then move this to the end of the routine. You could offer TV time as a reward for being ready on time with shoes and coat already on! If the toy basket is a source of distraction, get the hard parts like getting dressed done first. Position play at the end of your child's routine to encourage them to get through the routine quickly. If they are ready on time, they can have ten minutes' play or a snuggly story at the end.

You might also need to change where you do things to avoid pitfalls. If your child's room is full of toys, then you will want to keep them out of there if at all possible. Be creative. There is no reason why kids can't get dressed in the bathroom if their clothes are ready and waiting for them there. Teeth can be brushed in the kitchen sink if walking to the bathroom leads to an unhelpful detour to the toy closet. Design their journey through the house so they can complete all their tasks before meeting their priority for play.

Align your priorities, remove obstacles, and keep tweaking until you find the best route through.

HAND OVER CONTROL

Once you've reduced the tasks and thought through the sequence and location for your morning routine, put together a morning checklist or activity schedule for your child so they know what is expected from them. For younger children, this could be in pictures—a picture of a toothbrush, a picture of breakfast, a picture of some clothes, and a picture of shoes, all in the right order. You can get them to draw the pictures themselves. For a really young child, you might need to break that down into even smaller steps and focus on just one bit of the routine first—a picture of pants, a picture of socks, and a picture of a T-shirt. An older child's checklist would be more abstract—they might not need reminding to brush their teeth but they do have to check their timetable to see if they need their violin or gym clothes that day.

Set some ground rules about what is allowed (and not allowed) in the mornings. Lots of parents have a "no screens" rule in the mornings because TV and digital devices can distract children from the things they need to do. Screens might be handy for keeping a child occupied while you shower, but is the fight to get them off the device afterward worth it? Is there another way they could be occupied, or could you reorder the sequence?

Rather than nagging or bullying children through their routine, what we want is to motivate them to take responsibility for their own routine—a pull rather than push system. Rather than relying on discipline responses when things go wrong, the essence of a stress-free morning is to use motivation instead.

Remember your superpower? Use your attention to encourage your child to follow their routine. When the morning routine is going wrong, it's often because children are getting attention for exactly the behavior we don't want—for refusing to get dressed, for going slowly, or for sabotaging the routine in some other way. We nag, bully, or shout at exactly those times when they are not doing what we want. And although that is negative attention, it's still attention, and that negative attention can accidentally encourage children to repeat that behavior the next day. On the flipside, we often ignore children in the mornings when they are getting along and doing what we want them to do. We sneak off to get dressed while they put their clothes on nicely or check emails while they are eating their breakfast. The only way they get our attention is to misbehave or not cooperate.

The aim is to turn that around and give children attention for successfully completing the tasks on their morning list. To reward the right behavior with our attention rather than rewarding the behavior we don't want. That means giving them attention as a result of following their routine rather than as a response to sabotaging it. So try to catch your children following their routine and tell them exactly how much you like it. Use descriptive praise to tell them exactly what they have done right: "Well done for putting on your uniform so quickly, what a good boy!" Be warm, sincere, and enthusiastic. I know you still have to get yourself dressed too, but try not to ignore your child when they are getting it right. Before you sneak off to put your own clothes on, you could say, "You are doing so well putting your uniform on! If you can put your trousers on by the time I get back, I'll give you a big kiss!"

THINKING POINT

What motivates your child(ren) to do things they don't particularly want to do? What makes them feel proud of themselves? How could you hand over more responsibility for the morning routine to your child(ren)? What adjustments would you have to make?

USE MOTIVATION

You could also use rewards to kick-start a new routine. If you've made an activity schedule, then your child could get a tick, point, sticker, hug, or kiss for every task they complete on their schedule. For young children, a special sticker on their sweater for getting dressed by themselves can be motivation enough (smelly stickers stuck on the back of a toddler's hand work really well!). If getting into the car is an issue for your kids, they could get a special sticker for being in the car on time. For older children, you can use stickers or stamps on a chart that add up to rewards at the end of each day (with maybe a bigger reward at the end of the week) to keep them motivated. Tape the reward chart inside the car if that helps you get everyone out of the house on time or put it on the wall by the front door. But if stickers or stamps are not your child's thing, try marbles in a jar (or Lego pieces in a jar, or pennies, or ping-pong balls . . .) or use a ladder chart or a tally of points. You know your child best, so use what will motivate them.

Rewards do not have to cost anything—listening to their favorite song in the car, an extra bedtime story, a trip to the park on the weekend, baking cookies, or playing a game are all great ideas. The important thing is that your child is excited by the prospect of the reward and wants to make an extra special effort to achieve it.

It usually takes about three weeks for a motivation strategy to work. At the beginning, the rewards need to be earned frequently, so start with a low bar. If you think that the most you can hope for on the first day is that your child puts one sock on by themselves, then start with that. Make a big fuss about that one sock and reward them for it. Then, the next day, tell them they can have two rewards if they manage to put both socks on. Then move the goalposts so that they have to put two socks and a T-shirt on to get the same reward. Slowly keep moving the goal so that they need to work harder to earn each reward until eventually they are skipping through their whole routine and a new normal has been established.

You are unlikely to get exactly the right routine the first time, and children's needs change over time. So when you notice things are getting stressed in the mornings, don't be slow to go back to the drawing board. Have a look at who is doing what, where, and when the problems are occurring and see if you can rejig things. Most of all, be pragmatic—so if things are going wrong, try something different. Starting out right will make a difference to your whole day!

ACTION POINTS

- Analyze your morning routine. Make a list of all the tasks that need to be done, who does them, where, and in which order. Use a diary to track when/where problems are occurring. At which points are you giving your child attention? What are they doing when they get your attention? At which points do they meet their need for play?
- Try doing your morning routine in a different order or doing tasks in a different room and see what happens.
- Draw up a checklist or activity schedule to guide your child through their morning tasks. Use positive attention to reward them for completing each task. Position play time at the end of the sequence to encourage them to get through the tasks quickly.

8

Managing Sibling Conflict

I can't be the only parent who has gotten halfway through a dinnertime of squabbling children and wished I'd stayed at work instead. (And then felt guilty for thinking it.) There is nothing more guaranteed to leech the joy out of your precious family time than constantly bickering children. Whether it's continuous low-level guerrilla warfare, relentless competitiveness, or just ill-tempered flare-ups over specific issues, being called upon again and again to mediate between sniping kids is enough to tip the strongest parent over the edge. Sibling conflict can grate on your nerves, drain you of energy, and make you feel you are going home to a war zone—far from that connected and playful family time we had in mind! But it doesn't have to be that way.

Don't get me wrong, if you have more than one child, then the odds are 100 percent that those children will fight, argue, refuse to share, and wind each other up at some point or other. No child is born with a full set of social skills intact—they have to learn how to cooperate and negotiate and how to regulate their emotions when they don't get their own way. Practicing those skills with their siblings (and getting them wrong) is how they learn. Some squabbling is just inevitable. But it becomes a problem if it is the usual way children treat each other. When sibling conflict becomes ingrained it can quickly dominate the whole family dynamic, wearing down the nerves of already drained parents and sapping the fun out of family time. If sibling bickering is regularly sending you into fight (shouty parent) or flight (hiding in the bathroom) mode, then it's time to do something about it.

WHY DO SIBLINGS FIGHT?

According to evolutionary psychologists, sibling rivalry is a natural phenomenon. They compare the relationship between siblings to a survival of the fittest contest in which brothers and sisters compete for the limited resources available—what Darwinians call the evolutionary struggle for the milk supply. Though in the case of modern parenting, this usually manifests as competing for parents' attention rather than actual milk.

Other psychologists argue that developing a separate identity is a driver in sibling conflict. Children are "striving for significance" within the family ecosystem. They forge their unique identity by constantly comparing themselves to their siblings and trying to be different from them. That desire for difference often topples into belittling their siblings and wanting to be seen as "better" than them.

But simpler processes are probably at play too. Children's ages can be a big factor in sibling conflict. Children have different needs and understandings at different stages of development. So for example, a baby has no malicious intention when it takes an older child's toy, but the older child will interpret that action as "naughty." Older children can have a burning sense of injustice when younger children are treated differently or more leniently than they are. And they can resent spending time with younger brothers or sisters doing babyish activities that they have outgrown. Sometimes younger children feel jealous that their older brother or sister is allowed to do things that they aren't, such as having a later bedtime or staying out with their friends for longer. Those resentful and competitive feelings can easily lead to anger, frustration, or lashing out.

Now there's not much we can do about children's age gaps once they've been born (and any parent of multiples will tell you that having twins is not the easy way out!). But the good news is that one of the biggest factors in sibling conflict is actually us, the parents. Why is that good news? Because our own behavior is the one thing we can control and adapt. How we respond to kids' minor scuffles is a huge factor in whether those small conflicts stay at a manageable level or escalate into daily fisticuffs or attritional bickering. Parents frequently make sibling conflict worse by falling into patterns of behavior that, although sometimes successful in the short term, are counterproductive in the longer term. For example, if we end up shouting when we are frustrated with our children's behavior, we can't be surprised when our children copy that and shout at each other when they don't like what the other child is doing.

Remember the parenting holes from chapter 1? Sibling conflict is one of those sticky parenting issues where falling into the inconsistency trap really matters. If one day being mean to your brother is ignored but the next day it lands you on the Naughty Step, it's hard for children to learn to get it right. Unfortunately, consistency is difficult to muster after a long day at work when the kids are screeching at each other yet again. Instead we often end up veering from one extreme reaction to another. One day, when your patience level is at zero, the kids are sent to their bedrooms at the first sign of trouble. The next day, when we just don't have the stomach for it, we send ourselves to the bedroom and put a pillow over our ears to drown out the noise.

But the biggest trap of all when it comes to sibling conflict is paying too much attention to it (parenting hole number 4!). When you have a million things on your to-do list, it's so tempting to leave the children alone when they are playing nicely (and sneak off to get something done) and then come in with your full attention blazing once the children start to fight. We end up giving our attention to exactly the behavior we don't want (the fighting) and ignoring the behavior we do want (playing nicely). And as we know, children tend to repeat behavior that gets your attention. Children quickly learn that there is nothing more guaranteed to get mom or dad's attention than hitting their brother or sister. So they do it more often. Or they pull their hair or pinch them. Or call them a mean name. Or take their toy. And before you know it, family life descends into a negative dynamic in which the kids are constantly fighting, parents are constantly being drawn in to sort it out, and you are wishing you were elsewhere. Not the family life you want to come home to.

THINKING POINT

Is there a particular time of the day/week or a particular place or activity that always seems to result in your children arguing? If the answer is not obvious, keep a tally for a week. Mark when, where, and why arguments occur. How long is the shortest peaceful period?

ENCOURAGING COOPERATIVE BEHAVIOR

So what's the first rule for changing children's behavior? Define what "good" would look like and encourage your children to do a bit more of it. Brothers and sisters need to learn how to resolve their disagreements and behave in a polite, caring, and cooperative way with each other (for their sake and ours). So focus on teaching them how to get it right.

The best strategy for taking attention away from the wrong behavior and focusing it on the right behavior is to set some positive ground rules. Ground rules help children focus on what good behavior looks like so they can do it more often. If there is a particular sibling dynamic that you want to change, introduce a house rule to maximize alternative behavior. For example, if mean comments are the issue, then "Speak kindly" or "Use kind words" might be a good ground rule. Or if physical aggression is the problem, "Be gentle" or "Use gentle hands" would be appropriate. If shouting is the problem, then set a ground rule such as "Speak quietly" or "Use a nice voice." Choose words that your children will understand.

Go through examples of what behavior is within the rule and what isn't. Spend a bit of time discussing which words are kind and which words are not kind. With young children, take their hands and stroke your arm to demonstrate what "Be gentle" means or practice stroking their teddies in a gentle way. The children might like to decorate a poster and put the rule on the kitchen wall—whatever helps bring their attention to it. And remember, the ground rule applies to adults too, so no shouting if you have agreed on a rule about using a kind voice!

Once the rule has been set, be on the lookout for rule keeping rather than rule breaking. Acknowledge every kind word (*"Thank you for speaking kindly to your sister!"*) or every gentle act. Be enthusiastic and sincere—after all, you really do like that behavior and want more of it! Try to catch them being good and tell them exactly how much you like it. If they get it wrong (which they will—they are children, not robots), remind them what good behavior looks like and give them a prompt to get it right (*"Remember our rule about speaking kindly? Please try saying that again using kind words"*).

Ground rules can be for always (like house rules) or they can be just for a specific high-risk time when you know that there is a good chance that the children will end up fighting, like when they are playing a particular game or with a particular toy or when friends come to visit. Or in the car, or during day trips, or even just at certain times of the day like dinner or bath time when they always seem to bicker. Setting out a few clear, specific rules before children go into a high-risk activity can make a big difference. Then, as soon as possible, step in and praise them for sticking to the rules.

Turn your attention beam to maximum and use descriptive praise in a targeted way to encourage new behaviors. For example, "Well done for taking turns"; "Good girl, I really like the way you let your sister play with the toy when she asked for it"; or "Thank you for using words to ask for the toy. I could see you were getting frustrated with waiting, but you did the right thing and asked nicely. Well done." If fighting or arguing is particularly entrenched, then you might consider using a short-term reward chart to add some rocket fuel to the praise and shift the negative dynamic.

Reward charts are great for focusing your child's mind on the right behavior and motivating them to do more of it. Make sure you define clearly exactly what behavior you are looking to encourage, then divide the day (or evening) up into chunks of time. For every thirty minutes that your children are gentle with each other (that is, there is no fighting!), they get a tick, point, star, or sticker. At the end of each day, these might add up to a reward, with maybe a bigger prize at the end of the week. Start where your child can succeed. If you think they can only realistically go fifteen minutes without bickering, then start there. No stretch targets, please—aim for manageable stepping stones rather than giant leaps. We want them to get it right, experience the reward, do it again, and develop a new habit. Slowly move the goalposts so that they need to play nicely for longer in order to earn the reward. Then phase out the chart once a more peaceful dynamic has been established.

It's Not Fair!

How is it that all children bleat the phrase "It's not fair!" with the same musical intonation? We all know the tune. Usually children think being fair means dividing everything into exactly equal portions: having the same-sized slice of cake, exactly half the cookie, or precisely a third of the space on the sofa. And they will complain if they don't get their fair share (or more!).

Generally, "It's not fair!" is an empty accusation. (Hands up if you've ever been tempted to respond, "Well, life's not fair!") But if you take "It's not fair!" seriously, so will your children. And you will find yourself counting every sweet, measuring every crumb of food, and adding up every penny spent. It starts with counting the peas and ends with lawsuits about inheritance. I jest not. One parent I worked with got so far sucked into the "It's not fair!" game that when her tween son complained that she was spending more money on his older brother's rugby gear than on his arts sessions, she agreed to open a savings account for him in which to deposit the difference in spending. (To be fair, she was an absolutely brilliant parent, but her son could negotiate the hind legs off a donkey, and we all know what it's like to feel too ground down to keep resisting.)

As adults, it's really important that we don't reinforce children's sense of rivalry or join in with their competitiveness. Believing that there is a limited amount of pie to be shared intrinsically creates a winner and loser. If one child gets a little more, the others will de facto get a little less. Win–lose situations tend to provoke negative emotions, like fear, jealousy, and anger. The best solution is to give according to need rather than trying always to be equal. So when you are dividing up the apple pie for dessert and your child complains, "That's not fair, he's got more than me!" don't play the measuring game. Relate it back to what he or she needs. "Are you still hungry? Are you hungry enough for a whole slice or just a half?" Or when they complain about arts costing less than rugby, ask them if they'd like to take up rugby or perhaps another hobby instead.

Similarly, when your child tries to snatch your attention away from a brother or sister by saying something like "Mommy I want to show you something! Mommy! Mommy! You've been talking to Josh for ages!" you could say, "You're right. I'm spending time with Josh because he's stuck with his homework. I know it's not easy to wait but I also help you when you are stuck with things." Try to explain that when they have a genuine need then they will have their needs met and that is what really counts as fair. Not 50:50.

Try to convey that your love is not like a cake—it's not limited. Candles are a lovely way to do this. Gather the kids, dim the lights, and light a candle with a match (at a safe distance, of course!). Explain that this candle symbolizes the love you felt when your eldest child was born. Take a moment to say how much you love that child, why they are special, and how much you enjoy sharing their life. Then take another candle. Light the second candle using the first. Explain that this candle symbolizes the love you feel for your second-born child. Take a moment to say how much you love this child, why they are special, and how much you enjoy sharing their life. Ask the children to look at the two flames. Ask them if the first flame got smaller when it lit the second one and explain that's what a parent's love is like. There is enough of it to go around for every child. Keep going with the candles for as many children as you have, pausing to look at the undiminished flames and say how much you love each child and how special they are. The point of this exercise is not just to make all your kids feel loved, it's to help them understand that real fairness is a not a win–lose in which one person gets no more than another, it is a win–win in which everyone's needs are met.

Why Sharing Is Hard

Often as parents we resort to telling children to "share." But telling kids to "share" is pretty problematic because what does sharing actually mean? Different participants in any activity will often have a different view on what sharing would look like—just think how often adults struggle to agree on what counts as a fair share of things like time, money, and restaurant bills.

Little children are simply not capable of understanding an abstract concept like sharing. For toddlers, wanting exactly the toy that another child is playing with is part of their development process. We've all seen it happen. Your son is playing with his action figure. Your toddler spots it, drops her own toy, and demands to have the action figure. In a brave parental effort to encourage sharing and kindness (and avoid a toddler tantrum), you persuade big brother to give his little sister the action figure. He starts playing with a car instead. And your toddler instantly drops the action figure and wants the car!

Your toddler is not being awkward, she's taking her first steps in learning to play with another child. Young children learn through imitation—by watching and copying. As soon as they can sit up, babies are often fascinated by watching other children playing. Once they are toddlers, they want to join in. But toddlers haven't yet developed the social skills to engage in cooperative joint play. Their first step on the journey to learning those skills is wanting to play with the same toy as the other child. A toy often holds most interest to a toddler when another child is playing with it.

Rather than telling children to "share," I prefer the idea of helping young children learn how to cooperate. Children are not born knowing how to cooperate; just like riding a bike, it takes practice and a bit of falling off (and some children learn faster than others). With young children, it helps to break cooperation down into a less complex behavior such as "taking turns." We can teach young children to take turns by playing simple games with them like throwing and catching a ball or playing Snap! with a pack of picture cards. Make sure you use the vocabulary of turn taking as you do it. Say, "Your turn, my turn, your turn, my turn, whose turn is it now?" Reinforce this with lots of praise—"Well done for taking turns"—and give them some vocabulary to use when things go wrong, such as saying, "It's my turn now" or "Please can I have a turn?" Learning to take turns is the first building block for more complex cooperative play.

A quick word about toy ownership. Often parents can tie themselves in knots working out whether they should be forcing a child to share a toy that specifically belongs to them: "It's her favorite doll," "He really loves that bear," "She got it for her birthday." To get around this, lots of parents find it useful to have a particular place where each child keeps a handful of special toys that they don't have to share. A small selection of special toys that are put away when friends come around. Personally, I went a different route. When my boys were little, they shared a room. We didn't have a playroom and there wasn't room to swing a teddy in the living room, so all their toys were in their bedroom. And all their toys were stored together—all the animals in one crate, the dinosaurs in another crate, the soft toys in another, etc. (I like organizing!) Nobody knew which toy belonged to which child and neither of them had greater rights to play with a particular toy than the other. All toys were joint toys. Theoretically, they were allowed special rights to a toy on the first day they got it, but after that it just went into the pot. And to be honest, they seldom lasted a full day before the toy became joint property. Having two children of the same sex does make that approach easier, but it just goes to show that children will learn what we reinforce. And if we get protective when one child plays with a toy that we know our other child likes, the children will quickly learn to do that too. But if we give them the tools to negotiate and solve problems for themselves, they will find a way to compromise.

THINKING POINT

When you step in to resolve disputes between your children, what behavior are you modeling to them? Are you looking to judge who is right and who is wrong? Or who is to blame? Are you imposing a solution and expecting them to stick to it? Are you raising your voice? Are you preoccupied with making things fair and equal? How would you like them to resolve their disputes going forward? How does this goal relate to the behavior you are modeling?

Teach Them How to Solve Their Own Problems

Working parents are really good at solving problems—we get a lot of practice! Just getting children out of the house on time, dressed, fed, and with all the right equipment, is an epic feat of problem-solving ingenuity (at any time of day). But because we are so good at solving problems, it's tempting for us to step in and solve squabbling children's problems for them. To decide which child should have the toy. Or bring in the egg timer so they can take equal turns. But if we always do that, children don't learn to solve problems for themselves. And they will always need us to come and sort it out for them.

Time is the most precious commodity in a working parent's life. What if I said I could give you more time? Well, teaching children to solve their own problems gives you back time. Think of all the wonderful extra things you could do if you didn't have to mediate between your children! It might seem quicker just to go in and sort it all out for them or impose a solution, but once they can talk and have the rudiments of cooperative play (from about three years), teaching children joint problem solving is an investment of time that will reap huge rewards for at least the next decade of your family's life. Not to mention the benefits of problem-solving skills for children's social, emotional, and academic success.

Solving problems is so ingrained and habitual in most working parents' lives that we rarely stop and think how we do it. But all problems are basically solved in the same way:

1. We clarify the problem.
2. We come up with ideas for possible solutions.
3. We evaluate those ideas: What are the pros and cons of each?
4. We choose the idea we think will work best.
5. We put the chosen solution into action.
6. We review whether or not the solution worked or whether we need to try something different.

Usually, parents whiz through this process in a jiffy, skipping from problem to solution based on a whole bank of previous experience of what will work. When children are squabbling over a toy, it's pretty simple for parents to come up with a workable solution: "You have it for five minutes, then swap over" or "You have it today, then you can have it tomorrow." But if we come up with the solution, children don't learn how to solve disputes themselves. And because it's our solution (not theirs), we often end up having to police the peace to make it work.

If we want to encourage our children to solve their own problems, we need to slow down the problem-solving process, break it down into separate parts, and model clearly how to solve problems in a cooperative way. And we need to step back and not do it for them.

The next time your children are fighting over a toy or an activity try this:

1. Step in immediately—don't let it escalate into a fight. Help them to clarify the problem. Ask, "What's the problem?" Listen to what they say and summarize it back to them: "So the problem is you both want to play with the same toy."
2. Next elicit their ideas for solving the problem. Ask, "What ideas do you have for solving that problem?" It's guaranteed that each child will start with an idea that involves them having the toy in question, but persevere until they come up with some more options. Say something like, "OK, that's one idea. We need lots of ideas to solve problems." Help them take turns in coming up with ideas and only offer your own ideas if they are really struggling.

3. Once you have a little collection of ideas, prompt the children to evaluate those different solutions and think about the consequences of each one. "What might happen if you do that?" is a useful question here.
4. Ask them which idea they are going to choose—they must select a solution they both agree on. Be warned, they might agree on a solution that you think is terrible, unfair, or that just won't work. But that's OK. Even if you don't think it is the best solution, if they agree on it together then let them try it. Play is children's area of expertise and sometimes they really do have better ideas than adults! And when children make decisions together, the solutions often stick much better than if mom or dad impose a solution.
5. Let them try out their idea. (And be prepared to eat humble pie if it turns out you were wrong.)
6. If the solution breaks down and they end up squabbling again then go back and review the decision ("OK so it looks like that wasn't the best solution. Which other idea could you try?").

Remember, children don't have our bank of previous experience to help them solve problems, and sometimes they can come up with ridiculous ideas. Or be frustratingly slow. Or try to sabotage the process. If at any stage the process completely breaks down, you can always take the toy away for five minutes and try again later. But stick with it. Train yourself not to jump in with solutions ("I think you should do this") but to use coaching questions instead to help children find their own answers ("Have you got an idea that might help?"). Prompt them to evaluate their own ideas ("What might happen if you choose that idea?") and prompt them to make their own choice ("So which idea are you going to choose?"). And remember to let them make mistakes. You might be able to see clearly that a particular solution is a bad idea, but let them try it (unless there will be lasting damage) and find that out for themselves. Getting it wrong, reviewing what happened, and changing the plan will help build up that bank of problem-solving experience that helps them get better at it.

Obviously, this won't work with children who can't yet talk. But you will be amazed at the power of even a three-year-old to come up with great ideas! If you consistently go through this problem-solving process with children, they will gradually learn to solve problems cooperatively using words and ideas. Once they've gotten the hang of this method, you can slowly withdraw your support and reduce the prompts until one day you will hear them from another room going through the process all by themselves without you having to be involved at all.

Building a Family Team Spirit

You could extend this problem-solving approach by holding family meetings, especially if you have slightly older children (though younger children can also come up with brilliant ideas if you just ask them). Family meetings are a great way to help children learn how to express their needs and views appropriately and to take into consideration other people's needs and views. They are also a great format for agreeing on family limits and ground rules in a way that helps build a sense of your family as a team that is pulling in the same direction.

Family meetings can be as formal or informal as you like, but they should always be short. We're not talking full-length business meetings here! You can hold them regularly or just ad hoc to deal with specific issues, you can have someone taking notes if you like, you can have an agenda—it's a good idea to play around with formats to see what works for your family. (Our family meetings always involve cake.) The idea is to help children practice listening to other people's opinions and making joint decisions. You will need some simple rules, like "Everyone gets a turn to talk" and "Be respectful of other people's views and feelings." Learning to listen and talk about difficult topics and to disagree with each other in a respectful and calm way is part of the essential value and learning from family meetings.

> **"When children help to come up with solutions, they are much more motivated to make those solutions work."**

Collaborating with your children to tackle a problem creates goodwill and signals positive emotions and intentions, all essential characteristics of that win–win dynamic we are trying to create. Problem solving together and genuinely listening to each other's opinions strengthens family bonds: it makes everyone feel heard, understood, valued, and accepted. Inviting children to help solve a problem unpicks oppositional dynamics (parent versus child) and the negative thoughts and emotions that go with them. You are no longer in the territory of blame but of cocreating as a team. And even if your first family solution doesn't work, you have a framework for learning and trying again, which is a much happier place to be.

You can use family meetings for tackling practical problems (like arranging how four people can all use the same bathroom in the mornings without anyone being late), for agreeing on family limits and ground rules, or for stickier issues like how you treat each other. If bickering children are driving you into a frenzy, choose a calm moment to sit them down and discuss it with them: "Every time we sit down and have dinner, you two start arguing with each other and it makes the whole experience really unpleasant. I'd like to enjoy dinner time. Can we think of some ideas of things that would reduce the arguing and make it more pleasant?" It takes a bit of persistence, but family meetings can really help to build a strong sense of a family team and that everyone is on the same side, which makes the more difficult bits of parenting so much easier.

ACTION POINT

- Sit down together as a family and agree on some rules for how family members should treat each other. Rules must describe the behavior you want to see (not the behavior you don't want). Agree on some rewards for sticking to the rules and the consequences for breaking them.

9

Taking the Heat Out of Homework

If you are trying to dial down your work-based efficiency thinking and switch into curious, playful, empathetic parent mode, then homework presents a significant challenge. Because homework is a task. It's a task that needs to be done well. It's a task that needs to be done well within a deadline. It's a task that needs to be done well within a deadline and the outcomes of it will be judged by a boss (aka a teacher). It even has the word "work" in it. And there are targets to progress toward! Homework hits the sweet spot of a working parent's prefrontal cortex. It fires up our goal-focused neurons and sends us straight back into outcome-focused "efficiency thinking" work mode.

Homework needs to be done at exactly the wrong time for working parents. Our evenings are already overstretched—children want a piece of their parents, parents want to enjoy their children, everyone is tired and wanting downtime, but there is a meal to cook, bags to pack for the next day, clothes to wash, hair to wash, those gym clothes to find (again), phone calls to make, permission slips to locate and sign . . . and slap bang in the middle of that is homework. We know that our children have to do it, and we know that it is (at least theoretically) a valuable contribution to their development. But it's a chore that parents and children dread. And as a result, there is often very little joy in those home learning tasks. Which is a real shame, because joy is a key ingredient in children's learning.

> **"It's hard not to feel resentful when school has filled your precious family time with math problems."**

Homework (or reading or spelling for younger children) has become a battle-ground for many working parents. As parents, we know we have to balance the wish for our children to do well at school with looking after their wider well-being and emotional health. But when we are crotchety from work and our frontal lobes are in goal-focused efficiency mode and our child seemingly refuses to get their seven times table right (despite knowing it yesterday), nurturing their well-being while simultaneously meeting their school attainment targets doesn't always fit easily together. Supporting children to do well at school inevitably involves a certain amount of pushing. If you're lucky, your child learns to take pride in their efforts and sets about their homework willingly and diligently. But few children engage gleefully with every piece of homework they are set on exactly the day when it needs to be done. What if your child is tired? Or doing something else beneficial that they really enjoy, like drawing, ballet, or building a treehouse for ants? Or they just don't want to do all those extra catch-up sums because no matter how many sums they do, they really don't understand long division, and the more they fail the worse they feel?

We want to be good parents and we are constantly told that good parents read with their children and make sure they do their homework. So the temptation is just to push through and bully the kids into sitting there and finishing that piece of writing whether they want to or not. It's not the family evening you wanted (and it's not the family evening they wanted), but it has to be done, doesn't it?

WHAT'S THE POINT OF HOMEWORK?

Educators are divided on the merits of homework for younger children. Certainly some of the tasks my children have been sent home with over the years have appeared utterly pointless. My eleven-year-old son was once sent a word search to do for his French homework. The word search was in English. Now, I'm a qualified language teacher and I stared at that word search for a long time trying to fathom a French language learning objective and I couldn't find one. In the end, I just did it for him. (I'm not proud of that, and I'm not recommending it. But having already written a huffy email to school that week and been labeled a vexatious parent regarding a completely different issue, I decided that battling with neither the school nor my son was worth the effort.)

Parenting is all about choosing your battles. If we are going to go into battle over homework, let's be clear on what we are trying to achieve. For most parents, helping with homework is about helping children to do well academically and reach their potential. But is battling over homework actually the best way to achieve that?

One of the key pedagogical principles that underpins formal classroom education is that repetition aids learning. The more often a particular brain circuit is used, the stronger those neural connections become. I still remember my telephone number and postcode from when I was a child because it was drilled into me for safety. Similarly, I remember the alphabet song, the Lord's Prayer, nursery rhymes, and certain poems because many hours of my childhood were devoted to learning them "by rote": repeating them again and again until they formed a deep groove in my memory. The principle that practice makes perfect is absolutely sound, so getting extra practice via homework ought to help learning.

However, we also know that young children require fewer repetitions to learn something if they enjoy that learning, if it is playful. The one time my son got 100 percent on a science test, I quizzed him as to why it had gone so well (it was an unusual occurrence!). He recounted with great glee how his science teacher had walked out of a lesson on the solar system completely without warning. A baffled class of nine-year-olds had watched him tramp across the playing field loudly counting his paces until, 149.5 paces away, he retrieved a large picture of the sun from behind a bush and held it up. (The earth is 149.6 million kilometers from the sun.) He taught the entire solar system by physically positioning the kids in the playing field and getting them to run around each other holding on to long pieces of rope. It was the best fun my son had ever had in a science class and his best grade that year. Having fun means learning requires fewer repetitions. More fun, more likely to remember it, more learning.

Fun is all about flow and process, not outcomes. In contrast, when parents invest too heavily in the idea that homework is the best way to boost grades or improve reading levels, we can get sucked into focusing only on outcomes. It's a classic working parent efficiency thinking trap: "Homework helps children learn. My job as a good parent is to support learning, ergo I must force my child to finish all her math homework correctly no matter what the cost (preferably as quickly as possible so I can get on with something else)." Our focus shifts to the piece of work that needs to be produced, the book that needs to be read, or the spellings that need to be learned. The goal becomes completion. Or grades. We fall back into our goal-focused work mode and get intensely frustrated when our children go slowly, get their homework wrong, or can't remember something they knew yesterday. Or if they just find it hard to do something we consider to be something they "ought" to be able to do. Homework becomes a miserable experience and we try even more to hurry them through it. And our frustration all too easily comes out as blame, or it leaks out of us in a way that makes our child feel bad about themselves.

Our real homework priority as parents is not teaching children facts or knowledge but helping them to have the skills and attitude to become good at learning and to want to do more of it (whatever type of learning that might be). Supporting children's learning is not about handing in a perfect piece of writing or them getting great marks, it's about the learning process. Learning how to learn. (If it helps, don't call it homework, call it home learning!)

"The real point of homework is never the piece of work produced, it is the learning journey."

In fact, if parents focus too much on outcomes (grades), we can actively undermine children's learning. Kids who struggle to get good grades can label themselves as failures and just stop trying. And children who do get good grades can become fearful of failure and slip into an unhelpful perfectionist mode. Which is nuts, because failure is essential to learning! What we really want is a homework culture in which failure is not feared or frowned upon—getting things wrong is a natural part of learning and it should be celebrated: "I did that wrong—hooray—now I know what not to do! I learned something!"

Homework really ought to be about fostering children's enjoyment and curiosity, not ticking off a task. Take reading as an example. Every night your child brings home their reading book and you need to listen to them read and write something in the dreaded reading diary. Come rain or shine, interesting book or dull one, good mood or bad mood, your job is to force your child to read some words so you can fulfill your parenting obligation, write in that homework diary, and tick reading off your task list. No? What if our aim instead was to send children away from their reading session feeling like they wanted to do that again, to do it more often? If we stop seeing the point as finishing the book (or even learning to read) and start seeing the point as enjoying the moment of reading, that's an entirely different experience. When your child brings home a new book, don't rush. Spend time looking at the book's cover, asking questions, talking about the title and the pictures, predicting what the story might be about, and remembering other stories you have read that had similar titles or characters. In fact, if that is all you do and the book doesn't get read, I wouldn't mind at all! But when you do get around to starting the book, it will be in an entirely different frame of mind.

Helping our children to become good learners is the real point of homework so try not to overinvest in grades or outcomes. If homework is turning your house into a war zone, it's time to call a ceasefire. Step back, regroup, and look for the enjoyment. Challenge yourself to accept that you truly cannot control what your child does or doesn't learn. We cannot take learning and put it in children's heads (and trying to force it into their heads is counterproductive and quickly turns nasty). All we can do is optimize the conditions for learning and support them to engage with it.

HOMEWORK TRAPS FOR WORKING PARENTS

- Taking over so you can get it all done quickly.
- Saving it all up for the weekend.
- Turning it into a battle that goes on all evening.
- Focusing on short-term outcomes (finishing the task or individual grades) rather than long-term success (good learning habits and positive engagement).

MAKING HOMEWORK A HAPPY HABIT

Once you have accepted that you can't force cogent thoughts out of your child's head and onto a piece of paper (or vice versa), you can focus on what you actually can control. Which is providing a good environment for learning to happen. Ideally that means making learning fun and enjoyable. But let's be realistic—there will be occasional evenings postwork when your energy levels are on fire and your brain is fizzing with ideas for math games or funny voices for reading out loud. And then there will be lots of other days when all you want to do is collapse on the sofa. So rather than aiming for homework to always be fun (and beating yourself up for failing), aim for homework to become a not-unpleasant low-drama habit.

The best way to create a habit is by setting up a regular routine and sticking to it. In the long term, we want children to organize their own study sessions and take responsibility for their own learning; once they are teenagers, that will be really important. If you set up a regular homework routine with younger children, doing homework becomes a habit. At first, you will have to scaffold and enforce it, but over time, as long as you are consistent, homework will just become part of the fabric of their days and there will be far less battling.

So set a regular time for homework. Choose a time that suits your work/family schedule. The same time every day is ideal. But if clubs or extracurricular activities get in the way, then it's OK to have a few variations as long as these add up to a regular weekly schedule. The aim is small chunks of study time throughout the week rather than marathon Sunday afternoon sessions that ruin your weekend. Be careful to avoid scheduling homework at a time that interrupts children's play. If you have to tell children to stop playing and come and do homework instead, you are setting yourself up for a fight. Find a natural break when they are not playing. Straight after dinner is a great time (as soon as they get up from the table and before they are allowed to play again). You can involve older children in deciding when and how long the homework slot should be. It could be just fifteen minutes for younger children, thirty minutes maximum until they hit secondary school and exam preparations. And build in some homework-free days each week. So, for example, a homework schedule for a nine-year-old might be thirty minutes a day straight after dinner Monday to Thursday plus Sunday evening.

The rules of this study time are simple. If you have homework, you do it. No matter when it is due. If children can't finish a task in the allotted time, they can pick it up again at the next study period. If there are regular study slots throughout the week, deadlines can usually be met that way. If kids have no homework on a particular night, study time still goes ahead. They can read a book, do research around a subject, or choose an appropriate study activity. All recreational screens and gadgets in the house are off until the study time finishes. And there is no play. Children dislike a vacuum and they are much more likely to engage in a book if there are no alternatives! If there are younger siblings in the house who don't yet have homework, for them this is "book time," when they can look at books quietly, read with an adult, or maybe do some drawing in an exercise book. The aim is to develop a regular study habit that is age-appropriate and sets the groundwork for more intensive studying in later years.

Some schools run supervised homework clubs for older children straight after school (these double as childcare if you are lucky!). If your child goes to a childminder after school or is looked after by a grandparent, you might be able to work with them to incorporate a brief regular study time into the after-school slot—which will make your postwork shift much easier! With younger children, if necessary, study time can be done while out and about—such as practicing spelling or reading while sitting in the parking lot waiting for big brother to finish soccer club on Wednesdays. Be creative. The key is regularity and consistency. Experiment to find fifteen- or thirty-minute slots that work and then stick to them.

If you are really stuck, you can incentivize to get a regular routine going. If your child is totally resistant to homework or homework fights have turned into a source of resentment and dread, consider using a reward system as a short-term strategy to reset and get things back on track. Focus on rewarding process and effort rather than attainment. Agree on a system where children can initially earn points for simple process steps, such as telling you about their homework the day it is assigned or for sitting down to do homework at the right time. Gradually move the goal farther away so that points are given for completing fifteen minutes' work or for doing two days in a row, etc. Remember, rewards, just like business goals, need to be SMART:

- **Specific**: Be very clear on exactly what you are rewarding. Will sitting at the table with the book open for thirty minutes be enough or do they have to be able to describe what they have read?
- **Measurable**: Exactly how many minutes' study, words written, or sums completed will earn the reward?
- **Achievable**: If it's too big a stretch, then no amount of reward is going to succeed. Go for small, achievable stepping stones.
- **Relevant**: Focus on process (which children can control) rather than outcome (which they can't). Rewarding work accomplished rather than grades achieved is less likely to create anxiety or add to school stress. Good processes and effort will lead to improved outcomes.
- **Timely**: Small, frequent treats and incentives tend to be more effective than a final big reward if they do well on exams. Phase out rewards and replace them with just praise once a good study routine has been established. Encouraging children to reflect on their successes will stimulate self-motivation.

When it comes to actual homework tasks, make sure to step out of your goal-focused work mode and focus on process rather than outcomes. Your job is not to judge your child's performance but to encourage good learning habits. If children have good learning habits, learning will follow. So use encouragement rather than criticism and focus on effort and progress rather than attainment. Point out the things your child has done right rather than what they've done wrong. Acknowledge and praise when your child settles down to do their homework (especially if that has been a struggle before): "Well done for sitting down to do your homework, good boy." If you are leaving them to get on with it by themselves (which I recommend), show an interest and praise their efforts. If they ask for your opinion, or if you are checking their work, zoom in on the parts that are correct (especially if these are an improvement on previous attempts). And if you can see errors, rather than pointing these out, prompt your child to self-evaluate and to decide for themselves what they have done well and what they can improve. Ask them to predict what grade they think it might get, if they think their teacher will be pleased with it, or how their teacher will say it can be improved so that they get into the habit of evaluating their own work. Or tell them that you can see five spelling mistakes and challenge them to find them by themselves. Learning to reread, spot your own mistakes, and self-correct is an essential part of the learning process.

Remember, you are not the teacher. It is the teacher's job to evaluate your child's homework and decide whether they have met their learning objective. If you are concerned about your child's progress, go and speak to their teacher. If additional support is required, develop a clear plan with the teacher about what needs to be done and by whom. Don't use homework as covert ground to artificially inflate grades by improving your child's work for them.

> **"Think of yourself as providing a scaffold or framework to help your child plan and evaluate their work—what goes inside that frame must come from your child."**

It's fine to help, but don't do too much. Coach your child by asking questions rather than giving them the answers: "Do you have any idea what the answer might be? Can you remember anything from the lesson that might be help-ful?" Ask them to make an attempt before you assist and prompt them to use resources such as dictionaries, reference books, and the internet. Don't overdo it though. If they can't find the correct answer with one or two prompts, then step in and help. Try not to get frustrated if your child doesn't under-stand something after several explanations. Talk back to your own negative thoughts—your child is *not* doing it deliberately. Children all learn different things at different speeds. Prompt your child to review their learning materials to see if they can remember how to approach the task or encourage them to seek clarification from the teacher. Don't be tempted to extend the study pe-riod until they get it right—you will just end up feeling stressed and resentful because homework is invading your already overfilled family time. And your child will feel miserable. Just say, "Study time is up, let's come back to this tomorrow when our brains are feeling fresh."

If homework means reading a book with your child (or them reading to you), your focus should be on making it a pleasant and enjoyable experience (not on finishing the book). Be warm and welcoming. Show that you are pleased to be in that moment with them and communicate that you value the experience of reading with them. That will help your child to feel *good about themselves* no matter how well they do or don't read. Praise your child in a way that is descriptive and believable. Don't tell them they are a brilliant reader if that isn't true. The classroom is a very competitive and hierarchical place, and they will know exactly how their reading measures up against their peers. Comment warmly and sincerely on something very specific that they have done well this time or something they have done better than last time (even if it is only that they sat still) or on how hard they have tried.

THINKING POINT

When your child doesn't do as well on a piece of homework as you think they should, do you interpret that as

- a worrying predictor of their future success in life?
- a reflection of your success in parenting?
- a signal that they need to try harder and put in more effort?

All of these interpretations tend to lead toward negative thoughts, emotions, and actions—like blame, shame, fear, and battling. What alternative explanations might there be when your child doesn't do as well as you think they should? Could any of these be true?

- They didn't understand the task.
- They are going to take a little longer to master that learning/skill.
- They chose not to engage in the task.
- This skill may not be one of their unique talents.

Where would alternative explanations lead you?

Don't be tempted to use scare tactics. When a child doesn't seem to be putting in the effort, parents often resort to threats: "*You'll get moved down a table if you don't do well in your spelling test*" or "*You'll end up working in McDonald's.*" There is lots of evidence that these kinds of "fear appeals" increase pupils' anxiety and decrease actual results. I know you want your child to be successful and to reach their full potential so that every possible door is open to them. And when that doesn't seem to be happening, it can feel like their very lives are under threat. But there is a fine line between encouraging children and piling on the pressure. When parents push hard on academic attainment (with the best of intentions), children can interpret this as meaning they are not good enough. It becomes the bar against which they measure themselves, which can negatively impact their actual results and their self-confidence. Handing in a perfect piece of homework, moving up a reading level, or meeting an educational target by a particular date is never worth damaging a child's self-esteem, no matter how busy, stretched, or not in the mood for homework you are feeling that evening. Success at school can certainly facilitate success in life, but it is not the only route to happiness.

We can't force children to try hard at school, we can only encourage them to do so. One of the hardest things I have learned as a parent is that we have to parent the actual child we have, not the ideal one we wanted to have or the person we want them to become. Parenting a "must try harder" child who is frequently "off task" and doesn't put in the effort is intensely frustrating, but in the end there is nothing you can do to force learning into that child's head. If you set yourself that goal, you are setting yourself up for failure and conflict. The best we can do is to encourage children and provide the right conditions for good learning habits. That means prioritizing process over outcomes, accepting their mistakes, and encouraging them to learn through those mistakes. And waiting with hope and curiosity to see what wonderful path their life takes them on.

ACTION POINTS

- Set a regular study time of fifteen to thirty minutes for five days of the week. Remove all distractions. If there is no set homework, use the time for reading or further learning. Stick to the schedule for a fortnight, then sit down and review it with your children. What worked well and what might need to be adjusted?
- For a whole week, try approaching reading practice with the single goal of having an enjoyable experience.

10

Tackling Tech Time

Concerns about managing children's tech time are high on the worry list for modern parents. Newspaper headlines that scream "Screen-addicted children spend just sixteen minutes outside each day" don't help. Nor does the barrage of clickbait articles comparing social media to digital heroin (mostly to be found, ironically, on social media sites). Parents know that the digital world is a place where children can come to harm, yet that's exactly where children want to spend their time. And most advice on parenting seems to have been written in a golden age when wrestling smartphones off preschoolers wasn't a daily struggle.

For working parents, worries about children's tech time can be compounded by us simply not being there to supervise. Or by our lack of control over other adults involved in their childcare. Or by our own desperate need for that little bit of peace and quiet that screens offer. And then there's that niggling feeling that perhaps our own screen use might have gotten a little bit out of hand too.

Because, let's be honest, this isn't just about children—this is also about how tech has made inroads into every moment of adults' lives too and threatens to squeeze out things that we know are valuable, like reading books, playing with our kids, or talking to our partners. Family culture has been fundamentally changed by the technology in our pockets and our ability to log on anywhere, any time. Mobile communication means that more working parents are expected to field emails and answer work calls during nonworking hours, while mompreneurs and flexible workers try to stitch together laptops and home-working with simultaneous childcare. Hyped up and plugged in, we reach for our mobile phones even during the briefest of pauses—waiting for the kettle to boil or the satellite box to fire up, even sitting on the toilet. My teenager phoned me from the bathroom last week to ask me to bring him a towel. He had remembered to take his phone into the bathroom, but not a towel?!

We suspect that all this probably isn't good for our children or for us, but we are not really sure what to do about it. Where, and how, should we all be drawing the lines?

WHAT ARE SCREENS DOING TO OUR CHILDREN?

Most parents would love some certainty on the potential impacts of digital devices on children's health and development and some clear guidance on where to set safe and appropriate limits. Unfortunately, the experts don't have a clear or unified position. The sheer rate at which the digital world has infiltrated families' lives is outstripping the pace of research. Existing research on screen time is often based on watching TV, which in our new world of portable internet no longer seems the pertinent issue. And rapid developments in tech use mean that an eight-year-old today is having a very different tech experience from an eight-year-old five years ago. Good-quality research takes time, and on this issue it is lagging behind.

There have clearly been significant changes in children's lives in the past decade. Children in the United Kingdom are now physically safer than they have ever been and they are less likely to be in a car accident. Teenagers are less likely to have underage sex and they smoke less and drink less (whatever you might read in the papers). But then again, today's children are also less independent. They spend less time outdoors and are less likely to leave the house without their parents. And there is a lot of evidence that children are mentally more vulnerable. Children's mental health services are experiencing unprecedented demand. The number of children reporting suicidal thoughts is up, admissions to hospital for self-harm are up, and increasing numbers of children are showing symptoms of depression and anxiety. When I first started talking about children's mental health fifteen years ago, the standard ballpark figure was that one in ten children would have a diagnosable mental health condition at any one time. That figure has now gone up to one in nine.

Common sense might conclude that children's seemingly poorer mental health must be linked to that other big change in modern childhood: increased time on digital devices. But the research is less conclusive. There certainly are studies that link teenage depression to higher levels of internet usage, but whether excessive tech use leads to depression or depression leads to excessive tech use is less clear. And exactly what counts as "excessive usage" varies from study to study. We just can't say for sure what tech is doing to children's brains.

"The threat of tech is that children end up doing less of other more developmentally rich activities."

What we should be worried about, though, is what children are *not* doing because they are on tech. Children's tech use is increasingly displacing other activities that we know are definitely valuable to children's development and happiness, such as running around, face-to-face communication, and imaginative play. Tech has a tendency to expand to fill all the available time, it is habit-forming, and now that it is also portable, tech is an easy boredom-filler that's always in your pocket. Kids are less demanding when they are on tech and worn-out adults enjoy the peace that brings.

Young children learn best when they interact with their surroundings directly rather than through screens. It is through that repeated experimentation called play that children learn the fundamental principles of the universe—that water flows and objects fall to the ground, that some things fit inside other things, and that pebbles splosh and sink in water. No matter how many times a child sees a plane on the TV (or travels in one), it is by tying their dolls to makeshift plastic bag parachutes and throwing them down the stairs that they will understand how air holds up flying objects. And although a kids' TV program or YouTube clip might indeed help a child learn the alphabet by heart, it's a significantly impoverished developmental experience compared to interacting with a real person. Watching a screen doesn't involve taking turns in a conversation or learning to decode social and emotional cues. Screens expose children to learning, but learning is not simply about exposure—learning is about participation. The number of words a child hears aids their language development. But the number of conversational turns a child participates in matters more—this forms the foundation of their language, social, and emotional skills. (A conversational turn simply means "you say something, I say something, you say something, I say something.") The effects of a conversation-rich early environment can still be seen in a child's literacy skills even a decade later. The more tech children use, the less they converse face to face.

Tech use also tends to be sedentary. It involves sitting still, which means that children miss out on the health benefits and physical skills gained through moving around. Children's fitness levels have plummeted. The fittest children in your child's primary school class will have a level of fitness equivalent to the least fit children in your own school days. (Please read that sentence again so you truly understand the scale of this change.) The World Health Organization has linked children's screen time to rising rates of obesity and Type 2 diabetes, while the Royal College of Paediatrics and Child Health in the United Kingdom has warned that the blue light emitted by smartphones and tablets can impact children's health through disrupted sleep.

And it's not just children's own use of technology that impacts their development. Digitally distracted adults are less able to provide the connection, attention, and eye contact that help children develop healthy brains and essential life skills. Babies need eye-to-eye contact with engaged adult caregivers in order to regulate their stress levels and develop communication skills. Children learn by watching what their parents do. When they are unsure, they look at their parents' faces for information, connection, and reassurance. If parents are looking at their phones, that social learning is missed. Good family relationships are built not just on physical presence but on active mutuality. Peek into many homes and what you will see is everyone on their own digital device, even when they are in the same room. Parents and children may be spending more time in each other's physical proximity, but we are talking to each other less. And if you are trying to create a happy family dynamic, that really matters.

THINKING POINT

Which memories do you treasure most from your own childhood? Close your eyes for a few minutes and visualize yourself as a young child. How did you spend your time when you weren't at school? Which memories make you smile and give you a warm glow? How does this compare to the ways your children spend their time?

HOW MUCH TECH TIME IS TOO MUCH?

The lack of reliable evidence means that psychologists and healthcare professionals are divided on exactly how much tech time is too much for children. There is a general consensus that there is little or no value in screen time for children under the age of two and that screen time should be minimized under the age of five. But parents are left to make up their own minds about exactly what that looks like in practice.

The best way parents can support children's development is to make sure they have a balanced childhood that includes a wide variety of different play experiences to help them build their physical, social, and cognitive skills. To decide exactly where to draw the lines around children's use of technology, you'll need to bear in mind the following:

1. Not all tech use is equal. How much of your child's screen time is passive consumption (for example, watching TV) and how much is active and creative (for example, making music or animations)?
2. How does your child behave during and after screen time? Are they completely locked into the screen? Are they angry at being dragged away? Or do they naturally walk away and build on the screen ideas in unplugged play? If your child finds it really hard to push the off button, that's probably a sign that they need less tech, not more. Some children are more prone than others to the addictive quality of tech experiences.
3. What are they doing with the rest of their time? Do they have nontech hobbies and interests? Do they spend face-to-face time with friends? Do they get their recommended daily amount of physical exercise (three hours of physical activity a day for under-fives and sixty minutes a day of exercise for over-fives)?

If you're feeling flummoxed about where to draw the line, try keeping a tech diary for a week for every member of the family. Measure exactly how much time is being spent on different activities. (Be honest!)

Or do the ice cream test. When your daughter is badgering you to play a game on your phone, ask yourself, if tech was ice cream and she was pestering me for an ice cream would I give it to her? If the answer is no (because she has already had an ice cream that day or she's already eaten a chocolate dessert or two cookies), don't give her the phone. She will protest. But ice cream is an occasional food, not a staple, and our job as parents is to stand firm in the face of storms and make healthy decisions for our children until they can make them for themselves.

In the end, of course, it's not just children who matter. Parents need to balance the needs of the whole family. Sitting your toddler in front of a TV or tablet for thirty minutes is not going to support their development (no matter how much the app's marketing messages tell you otherwise). But if that same toddler has been winding you up all day to the point of no return and the alternative is that you lose your temper or parent harshly, please turn on the TV. Lots of working parents use screens strategically to facilitate the smooth running of family life—like being able to take a shower or cook a meal without tripping over a child. Just look out for drift and be alert to the tendency of tech to expand to fill more and more time. It is surprisingly easy to start by introducing thirty minutes of *Peppa Pig* or iPad time so you can make dinner and find yourself sleepwalking into a situation where the TV goes on all evening after school and your ten-year-old is glued to a console.

TAKE A WHOLE-FAMILY APPROACH

With tech, as with everything, the first rule is to be a good role model. Setting limits around technology is best done through a whole-family approach. Children will be the first to call you a hypocrite if you curtail their tech use while merrily checking your own phone! Aim for a family life that includes breathing space for everyone by creating tech-free places in your home and tech-free slots in your schedules. These might be physical tech-free spaces like a "no screens in bedrooms" rule, no tech use allowed in the car (the car is a great place for talking!), no phones at the dinner table (ditto!), or no screens upstairs. The aim is to create zones where parents and children engage with each other and give their brains a digital break. And children will quickly learn to fill those spaces with diverse activities.

Depending on your schedules, you might decide on tech-free times of the day or tech-free days of the week. Lots of parents have a "no screens in the mornings" rule. But you could opt for no TV Monday through Thursday, tech-free Sundays, a digital detox Sunday afternoon, or no tablets except on the weekends. A screen-free hour before bed is recommended for all children by the Royal College of Paediatrics and Child Health. Experiment with different tech-free formats to see what works for you, but make sure you make conscious decisions about where to set limits to avoid drift.

The exact formula of a whole-family approach will vary from family to family, but the rules must apply to everyone and they must be consistent. It's a great idea to get older kids involved in setting those limits via a family meeting. Most of the time, parents give in to tech use because we are worn out from battling it again and again every day. The trick to containing tech use successfully is to agree to the rules and be 100 percent consistent in applying them. The more consistent you are with your rules, the fewer draining daily battles you will have. Set low limits when children are young and then move them only gradually as they get older. And don't believe children when they tell you that *all* their friends have an Xbox in their bedroom! There will always be parents who make different decisions from you, and that's OK.

THINKING POINT

Keep a family time tech diary for a week. Make a note of every time you and your child(ren) use a screen in the hours when you are with your kids and not working. Be honest and include every minor surf on your phone. What proportion of your children's waking hours does this represent? How does it compare to the amount of time they spend talking with you or doing physical exercise or running around play?

Cultivate habits that create as many tech-free spaces as possible and a family culture in which tech is not invasive. Challenge yourself to leave your phone at home on days out. (If you are worried about missing a photo opportunity, the research shows that we actually make more vivid memories when we don't photograph an event!) Prioritize family activities where tech just isn't an option. Go for a walk, take a bike ride, or pack a picnic. Take a ball to kick around in your local park. Sign up for canoe lessons or surf school or just go swimming at your local pool if you're not an adrenaline nut! Visit a museum, a castle, or a city farm. Climb a mountain (or just a hill). Build a fort out of fallen branches in the woods or go on an insect hunt. Collect stones with your little one and bring them home to wash and decorate. Personally, I'm a huge fan of camping with kids (though I appreciate that not everyone shares my passion for a weekend without a warm shower or a good night's sleep!). Find a campsite with no WiFi or electricity so there is no arguing about which child wants to watch what on which device. When the sun goes down, the choices are snuggling up with a flashlight and a book, a game of cards, or just talking about the day. If you insist on a comfy bed and a functioning kitchen, then book a camper or holiday cottage without WiFi.

And when you are at home, try to maintain some distance between yourself and your phone by leaving it in another room so you can't see the incoming messages. Or turn off app notifications so it flashes and burbles less. The less your child sees you interacting with your phone, the less they are going to want to play with it too. And when you do use tech during family time, try to make it communal and a shared experience. Rather than everyone retreating to interact with their own devices and not talking to each other, you could have some family-based tech experiences such as a family movie night or a computer game tournament.

Now, let's be realistic. I'm not suggesting that you come home after a day at work and fill every evening with creative play ideas to keep your kids off tech. Remember, it's not your job to stop your children from ever being bored. Try to make the shared family activities you do together as interactive and tech-free as possible. And for the rest of the time, once the children's tech time limit has been reached, just put the tech away. Stand firm and let the children get on with finding something else to do.

If you feel like tech time has got completely out of hand, you can always press the reset button and take all tech away. They won't like it at first, but children abhor a vacuum so they will find other activities to fill that time. I once did an experiment with a group of families who were challenged to reduce their children's tech time. The really brave ones took TV or tablets away completely. And they were also the families that saw the most noticeable results—siblings arguing less and playing more cooperatively and imaginatively, a reengagement in other activities like crafts, and a calmer household. All of the parents reported that as long as they stuck to their guns (and they also put their tech away), within a week the kids stopped pestering them to give the tech back. So don't be frightened to push that reset button. You can always reintroduce tech slowly and keep it on a more reasonable footing.

Setting limits and creating tech-free spaces within family life definitely takes effort, but once rules are established, you won't have to fight about it every day. If you introduce a new rule that says no screens or tech between 6:00 p.m. and the children's bedtimes, you can expect some pushback to start with. Habits can take time to change. But be consistent and the rule will stick, especially if the adults in the house are sticking to it too. If you fall off the wagon and find that tech has crept up on you all, just try again. The developmental benefits of a well-rounded childhood are huge, not to mention the health benefits for you of extra exercise and screen-free relaxation. And the memories you make as a family will be priceless.

USE A TECH TIME BEHAVIOR CONTRACT

If you have found yourself in a bit of a negative rut of daily battles over tech or you are constantly taking devices away as a consequence for poor behavior, you might want to think about turning things around and positioning tech time as dependent on other conditions being met first. One way to do this is through a behavior contract. Behavior contracts are a useful tool for managing tech time with older children (eight years and over). They set out clearly in advance what behavior is expected, what rewards or privileges will be earned by sticking to the rules, and what the consequences will be for misbehavior.

If spending too much time on tech (and not enough time on other activities) is the issue, think about setting a low/minimal tech time allowance and offering your child the opportunity to earn extra tech time through other positive activities. This is a great way to help maintain a balanced childhood for tweens. Set out the ways your tween can earn additional tech time in a behavior contract. For example, you might give a basic allowance of thirty minutes of screen time every day but agree that they can earn an additional thirty minutes of tech time for the weekend for every two hours of sports or physical exercise they participate in that week. Or you could set the daily limit at fifteen minutes and stipulate that they can earn an extra fifteen minutes for that evening if they complete all their homework or do thirty minutes of studying/reading. Think about which specific nontech behavior or activities you want to encourage in order to achieve a better balance and then position tech as a positive consequence for those happening. The contract can be written down and signed by parent(s) and child.

The exact behavior you stipulate will depend on your tween's particular challenges. Being physically active, studying, helping out around the house, and participating in family activities are all good themes for a behavior contract. If your daughter has a massive tantrum every time you turn off the tech, then rather than constantly taking tech away, use extra tech time as a motivator for coming off tech without a fuss. Set an appropriate (low) daily allowance and explain that if she switches off the tech without any arguments when the time is up, she can bank an additional ten minutes for the next day or for the weekend. But if there is an argument, she will lose ten minutes from the next day's allowance. You can help older children develop self-control by moving toward a weekly tech allowance and giving them a bit more freedom to choose exactly when they use their tech time so they practice making choices about allocating their time and turning it off themselves.

Review the behavior contract after a week to ensure that it is working and tweak the terms if necessary. If you are consistent, and if your tweens are motivated by tech time, they will be prepared to do the things necessary to earn it. The key is in setting a basic allowance low enough that they want to top it up (but restricting the maximum top-up time available to an acceptable level). Don't worry if you get it wrong at first, just review and adjust the contract. If you can make it a collaborative process in which your child feels their ideas are being taken on board, all the better. Make sure you define precisely what will earn the extra tech time—if you are too vague, you are guaranteed to end up in an argument about whether or not they have done enough to get the payoff! And like all reward systems, behavior contracts only work if parents are consistent and the system is actively monitored. There's no point setting rules if you can't supervise whether your child is sticking to them. Keep devices out of bedrooms and confined to shared family areas where you can see what is going on. And if there are other adults involved in your children's childcare, you'll either have to get them on board with the rules or (if it's impossible to get Granny to turn off the TV) set rules that accommodate those blind spots (such as weekday TV only allowed at Granny's house!).

> **"Ultimately, our aim is for children to learn to self-regulate their relationship with tech in a healthy way."**

In days gone by, parents were able to let unavailability do some of the heavy lifting in helping children learn to manage their relationship with tech. In the past, children's TV was only on for a few hours a day. If you were out, you missed it. It's not so very long ago that the first video recorders arrived in homes (I am old enough to remember them!), but even then setting up the tape was such a hassle, you'd only bother for recording something special. Now, TV on demand and a live pause button mean that children never have to grapple with the disappointment of missing a moment of their favorite program, and internet access via mobile phones makes their favorite characters or games available at all times, in all formats, in every location. Learning to turn off tech when it is always available at the touch of a button is a much harder lesson.

Younger children will need parents to be their external regulators. Some children will learn to self-regulate their tech use easily while others get truly locked into devices and find it harder to leave them alone, and you'll need to modify your approach accordingly. Learning to switch off will be much easier for them if you can model a healthy relationship with your own tech. And tuning off from your phone will make it much easier for you to tune in to your children. You might just find yourself with precious extra time that you didn't know you had.

ACTION POINTS

- Designate some tech-free places in your home and/or some tech-free time in your family schedule. These must apply to adults as well as children.
- Have a family meeting to come up with fun low-tech activities you can all do together. Include big things that take a whole day/weekend and little things that only take half an hour. Only include activities on the list if everyone agrees. Set a target for when you want to have tried them all by.
- Create a "Kids' Boredom Kit" for little ones of interesting things that fit into your bag/pocket that you can use to entertain them while you are out and about (without reaching for a smartphone). Buff up on some new word games for bored moments.

III

BALANCING WELL-BEING AND WORKLOAD

11

Taming Your Stress Monster

Setting some clear ground rules and focusing your attention on what children are getting right is a win–win: it makes you feel good, it makes children feel good, and it encourages them to get it more right more often. Managing children's behavior positively will go a long way to building a family life that is low on conflict, high in warmth, and good for your children. But positive parenting strategies can never succeed if you are too stressed from juggling work and family to manage your own hot spots and triggers. And I don't know about you, but I want a little bit more from life. My children's learning and development means a lot to me, but I also aspire to something greater. I want a family life that meets my needs too, which is not all about the kids.

So far we have looked at changing the way you think about parenting and about your children in order to understand their behavior better. We have thought through ideas about how you can switch out of work mode and connect with your child in those little bits of time around the edges of work and how you can navigate difficult parts of the day and maintain boundaries without battles. But somewhere in the middle of all this is you—a person with strengths, needs, dreams, values, and talents. Children are enormously demanding, but putting yourself on hold (while running at full tilt) for eighteen years is not an option. Being a successful working parent means, somewhere in the mix, looking after yourself and designing a family life in which you can thrive. Because you really matter.

Work can contribute both positively and negatively to stress. Our work lives can be a source of personal support and self-esteem, an anchor into the adult world that provides frazzled parents with much-needed perspective and social connection. But work can also create pressure to be constantly busy, constantly "on," rendering us permanently hyped up and drained at the same time and disconnected from the patience, empathy, and playfulness we need for a successful shift into parent mode. To many parents, working part time looks like the ideal solution, but the number of hours you work isn't really the deciding factor. Of the times when I have been my most distraught and cranky as a parent, one was when I was not working at all (being a stay-at-home mom with a baby and a toddler left me exhausted and sometimes, frankly, unable to face the day!). And one was when I was working part time (in a heavy-end child protection role where I never quite succeeded in letting go of the fear and responsibility of the day job). It isn't the exact number of hours you work that enables a successful work/life shift, it is how well you manage the stress associated with those hours.

Learning to stand down your efficiency thinking will go a long way to increasing relaxation and lowering your stress levels. Efficiency thinking is inherently stressful because you are always working toward something out of reach, always policing the moment to make sure that each and every goal is achieved. Stepping out of work mode and into your child's shoes and investing time in playfulness will bring huge rewards of energy in return. But the work/parent switch will only succeed if you learn to tame your stress monster and build your own well-being into your family life.

HOW STRESS IMPACTS PARENTING

You can spot a pushed-over-the-edge parent a mile off. There is a wild look in their eyes. Ridiculous things come tumbling out of their mouths (a little too sharply) as they frogmarch their children through the parking lot ranting that they have "HAD ENOUGH! For goodness sake, how hard can it be? I've told you so many times . . ."

We've all been there.

Stress fundamentally gets in the way of a successful work/parent switch. It undermines our efforts to be the parent we want to be—that loving and calm parent who doesn't snap or lose their cool. Stress drains us physically, sapping the energy we need to be playful and to connect with our family at the end of the day. And it drains us mentally, making our thoughts race and taking us out of the present moment, where it's harder to tune in to our children's signals. Stress hijacks self-confidence, picking away at our self-belief with niggles, fears, and worries, leaving us wound up, irritable, and far more likely to snap at our children.

"Stressed-out parents find it much harder to provide the loving warmth and consistent boundaries that children need to thrive."

Stress is the body's natural response to danger. When faced with a threat, humans trigger a short circuit in our nervous system through which we bypass the thoughtful front regions of the brain and go directly to the more visceral back brain regions that govern our survival instincts. We become instantly more alert and ready to react to the slightest signal. This hyperalert, hyperreactive fight-or-flight mode has a really important role in keeping us alive in moments of danger. But in the face of a screaming toddler or a tantruming tween, a fight-or-flight response (though understandable) is not especially helpful. It turns children into an enemy to be fought or escaped from and prevents us from engaging our more reflective brain regions to see that this situation is not a threat that needs to be defended against but is simply a child being a child.

Working parents spend a lot of our day having our stress response triggered. Modern employment contracts are essentially competitive—we are fighting for our professional lives ("I must get that project completed on time. It must be good. I mustn't fail. My career depends on it"). Everything that gets in our way becomes a threat—inept colleagues, malfunctioning tech, other commuters—triggering a surge of fight-or-flight adrenaline. That fight-or-flight button gets pressed again and again during our working day, so insistently that it can get stuck permanently on and it gets harder and harder to turn it off. And when every day is lived balancing on a stretched-out wire trying not to drop anything, chronic stress becomes the norm. It begins to feel like this is the way it always is and always will be.

I confess, when I am stressed, it's usually interactions with my children that make me realize there is a problem. I find myself excessively haranguing my son about an untidy bedroom or a spilled yogurt or reaching for ridiculous consequences in response to minor misdemeanors ("That's it, that's the final straw, I'm taking your console and putting it in the garbage!"). Or worse, I am unable to stop a bitterly negative interaction because my real agenda is offloading my own mood, not engaging with my son's responses.

Stressed-out parents overreact. Stress activates neural networks specifically designed to react at lightning speed, so stressed parents are inevitably much quicker to jump to judgments without stopping to think or listen. Our big reactions are easily triggered, often by small events, and we fly off the handle. And because stress activates those parts of the brain most alert to threats, we become much more likely to perceive other people's intentions as negative. Stress primes our whole nervous system to interpret actions as aggressive, making us quicker to assume that our child has done something deliberately to annoy us (when actually he was just being a child). A trigger-happy fight-or-flight mechanism makes calm parenting even more difficult, adding to the cycle of stress and ensuring that nobody is heard and nobody's needs are truly met.

Being a working parent is challenging and we all feel the strain sometimes. But when we fail to manage stress or allow it to become chronic, it drains us of the capacity to build sensitive emotional bonds and can end up undermining the whole family's well-being.

DECIDE WHAT'S IMPORTANT

I can't really advise you on reducing your work stress. I don't do your job and I have no idea about the demands it makes or the flexibilities that are/are not on offer. I'll have to leave that to you. All I would say, though, is that if stress from your job is undermining your mental health, don't ignore it, do something. But when it comes to the stresses created by trying to be part of a modern family, I do have some ideas. And the first of these is "do less."

Trying to fit too much into your family time compounds work stress and makes it much harder to switch out of task-focused efficiency mode and be that process-focused parent who enjoys the moments. So why do we do it? Sometimes parents try to squeeze too much into our nonworking hours because we think that doing so is enabling or necessary—that we need to accomplish all these tasks and get everything done in order to create the home life we want. But then we find ourselves so busy creating the right conditions for life that we have no time for enjoying it. Sometimes it's a case of conflicting priorities. As parents, we want the best for our children. We feel like we will be letting them down if they miss out on a single birthday party, karate tournament, or clarinet session. But by trying to shoehorn too much into limited time we squeeze out other essential happiness-building ingredients like relaxation, play, and connecting time.

If you really want to tame your stress monster and create a family life you enjoy, you will need to challenge some deeply held beliefs, question the things you regard as givens, and prioritize according to your own goals (rather than other people's). And that means deciding what's really important.

Trim Your To-Do List

If getting through all the things on your at-home to-do list is getting in the way of spending time with your children, it's time to have a long hard look at that list. As a first step, write down everything you are trying to fit into your family time. Seriously. On a Sunday night, write down everything you have done that weekend—every meal prepared, every piece of homework checked, every bit of DIY attempted, and every phone call made. Make the list as complete as possible. For good measure, throw in all the tasks that you had hoped to get done but didn't get around to. Check that this is a typical list and add in anything that you usually do that hasn't been captured. The aim is to create a master list that represents all the things you are trying to squeeze into your nonworking hours.

For each and every task, ask yourself those four key prioritization questions:

1. Does it need to be done at all?
2. Does it need to be done by me?
3. Does it need to be done so well?
4. Does it need to be done now?

Prioritize ruthlessly. Cancel, delegate, outsource, park for the future, and banish perfectionism. You cannot do everything—and you certainly cannot do everything perfectly. Pick what really matters and find an alternative solution for the rest. You might want to coach the under-sevens soccer team, but can you realistically fit it in? What will be the impact if you do it? What won't you be able to do if you do it? Who will be most affected? What difference would it make if you did it next year instead? Or if you were just a parent helper rather than a coach?

If the outcome after all that scrutiny is that coaching the under-sevens is truly a priority, that's great. If it is something that connects with your strengths, exercises your talents, makes you feel good, and leaves you elevated and inspired, then it will undoubtedly increase your sense of well-being and is 100 percent worth doing. If an activity resonates with greater meaning and gratification than the time it takes up; if it energizes you and involves learning, connecting, and reaping rewards from effort; and if, even better, it hits the sweet spot of also involving exercise and kindness and helps you to feel like you (and feel happy with who you are), then give it more time, not less. These are the ingredients that build happiness and you want as many of these on your list as possible.

But don't just do things because you feel you ought to. Or because your friends do it. Or because your mother-in-law might judge you otherwise. Or because you have always done it that way. Don't do the things that leave you feeling drained, glum, or angry; find other solutions for those—cancel, delegate, postpone, or botch. Or find a way to do it differently. Not everything can be a priority, so be focused and keep going through that list to find something that can be ditched or outsourced.

Some things will always have to be done, like making meals and washing clothes (not many of us can afford to outsource everything!), but make sure you share household tasks fairly—and that includes with the children. Don't run around clearing up after your children after a long day at work, doing things for them that they could do themselves. Teach your children to be independent and expect them to contribute and do things for themselves. Whether it's making their own beds, preparing their own lunchboxes, or washing their own hair, if they are doing it for themselves that will be one less thing for you to do. You'll need to invest time in teaching them new skills (and you'll have to accept that they might not do it as well as you). But if you don't insist that they take responsibility for basic tasks, you'll still be buttering their toast and packing their school bags when they start secondary school. Grinding ourselves down doing menial tasks for children who are old enough to do those things for themselves is not an act of love, it's an act of developmental sabotage and means you will never have enough time to enjoy being a member of your family. So get ruthless with that to-do list.

THINKING POINT

Think about how you spend your nonworking hours. Which activities make you joyful? Which activities energize you? Which activities feel most meaningful and gratifying? When do you feel most like you?

Focus on Big Goals

If you really can't find anything to cross off your list, try some outcomes-based thinking to help you prioritize. Get another sheet of paper and write down your big goals for family life (no more than three)—the fundamentally important things like "Raise my children to be kind," "Create happy childhood memories," or "Make a difference to the world." Make sure you identify the goals that truly resonate with your dreams and values. Then brainstorm a list of actions that would *directly* contribute to achieving those goals. Like doing something kind for a friend in need, climbing a mountain with your children, or campaigning on a local issue. How much of your time do you currently spend doing those activities? How many of the tasks on your to-do list are actually making a *direct* contribution to those big goals (and how many are getting in the way)? Are you filling your time with proxy tasks that give you the illusion of making a difference or being on top of things without actually being meaningful? Does washing the car once a week make a direct contribution to your big goals? Or is it one of those boulders you use to shore up against feelings of chaos or incompetence? What if you spent that time doing something more directly happiness-building instead? How would that feel?

"When you are directing your limited time and energy toward activities that are truly meaningful to you, they give back energy."

Prioritize meaningful activities and have reasonable expectations of what you can fit in. You might still be tired all the time, but it will be a much better tired! And if you can't quite let go of other people's expectations, take a cue from a parent I know who gave up vacuuming for a whole year. To save face, she parked her vacuum cleaner by the front door and would gesture at it casually when visitors came in, saying, "Sorry about the mess, I was just about to vacuum." (But she never actually did!)

I used to force myself to get all the household stuff done as soon as I got home from work so that I could sit down and watch TV for an hour to unwind before bed. Slowly, I learned to sit down and do my unwinding with my tween when I first came home. We'd often end up talking about ourselves or our day or just silly stuff. I'd still get to unwind and, OK, sometimes not all the jobs get done. But they never used to all get done anyway! And the time with my son was priceless.

SELF-CARE MOMENTS FOR BUSY LIVES

Children will always be hard work, especially if you are outnumbered by them. Dealing with children at their worst moments, when they are tired, emotional, or stuck in bickering mode, is not fun. And when you are also at your worst moment, clouded with tiredness from a day at work, it's doubly difficult. Being calm and consistent in those tough times requires bottomless internal strength. If you want to create a positive family dynamic and enjoy your family time, it is absolutely essential that you take time to top up your own internal resources. Be ruthless with your to-do list, yes, but make sure that it's not always your "me time" that loses out to the time pressures.

When your life is timed to the second between drop-offs and pick-ups, even a few minutes of self-care can seem unattainable. But that's a classic efficiency thinking trap: looking to save the minutes but ruining the moments. Parenting is a marathon not a sprint so you need to manage yourself with an eye on the longer term. Treat yourself like an athlete. Recovery time and rest days are what enable you to keep running. Being a working parent is so much easier when your own needs are being met. Taking time out to relax and to see friends and spending time doing things designed around your interests (not just the kids' needs) are all essential for your well-being.

Working parents are quick to jettison our own relaxation just because there is so much to do and so little time, and something has to give. But once we have deprioritized our own well-being often enough, we start to feel guilty about taking time out for ourselves and we construct our days around supporting our family instead. And then the people around us forget to support us because they've gotten used to us always helping them. Yet neglecting self-care is ultimately self-defeating. Because when we don't look after ourselves, we quickly undermine our ability to look after others or to be the calm, empathetic parent we aspire to be. And by deprioritizing ourselves, we deplete our ability to manage stress, which makes being a working parent harder, not easier.

I'm not suggesting that you take every weekend off or head for a spa day once a week (though please do that sometimes!). Even just tiny bits of self-care can make a big difference. Looking after yourself is about small daily choices and little snippets of time rather than just occasional big breaks. Make yourself a list of quick-win self-care ideas that you might be able to fit into down moments (I'm a working parent—I love a list!). Here's my selection of one- to sixty-minute self-care ideas for busy parents:

- **Go for a walk** (with or without the kids). A bit of fresh air, a change of scenery, and gentle exercise can have a wonderfully rejuvenating and meditative effect. It also requires virtually no preparation. Even just a few minutes' walking is good for your well-being, especially if it also involves connecting with nature.
- **Daydream**—about happy things, such as a really enjoyable vacation or a brilliant day out. Close your eyes and try to re-create a happy moment in as much detail as possible in your head. Visualizing it will release all the positive thoughts and feelings associated with that memory and bring

them into the present. (This is a great one for the train journey home from work!)

- **Get some exercise.** Whatever type of exercise does it for you—run, swim, gym, bike—preferably something quick that you can just head out and do spontaneously when you have a spare half hour.
- **Just breathe.** You know, you don't have to do anything at all. A few minutes just focusing on your breathing is deeply relaxing. Close your eyes and breathe in through your nose for a slow count of five, hold for a count of three, then exhale through your mouth for a slow count of five. Pause for a count of three then repeat. Your cortisol levels will reduce almost instantly.
- **Connect with a significant other.** Investing snippets of time in your special relationships pays dividends. Take a minute to send a sexy text to your partner, a funny joke to your sister, or a "Do you remember when . . . ?" memory to your best friend.
- **Dance,** or just listen to music if you are not a dancer. Grab your phone and instead of scrolling through social media find a song from your past that you have always loved. The type of song that makes your heart soar and your hips wiggle. And dance like no one is watching. Do it in the garden, the kitchen, or the shower if you are shy, but let loose. Day by day add the best songs to a playlist and you'll always have five minutes of energizing music in your pocket.
- **Stretch.** Stand up straight, feet firmly planted on the ground (bare feet are great for this), and make yourself as tall as possible. Imagine there is a string gently pulling your head upward while heavy shopping bags are weighing your arms downward. Learn a few yoga stretches for odd moments of the day.
- **Sit outside.** I am lucky enough to have a garden and the best investment I ever made was a comfy place to sit in it. Even in the winter (as long as it's not raining), I will grab my coat and a cup of tea and sit and watch the robins darting around and listen to the birds sing. A bench in a local park would do just as well.
- **Find a ray of sunshine, and turn your face to it.** Savor the warmth and feel the air move on your skin.
- **Practice a bit of mindfulness.** Wherever you are just stop what you are doing and bring your attention fully to the present moment for a few minutes. Focus on your least dominant senses. For example, close your eyes. What can you hear? What can you smell? If thoughts intrude, just recognize them as thoughts, let them pass, and bring your attention back to your senses.

- **Catch up on a podcast**—maybe something funny, or a radio play. I seldom get the chance to listen to a full radio show without being called away by kids or work so I download them and then, when I have a spare few minutes, I sit back with some headphones and listen properly.
- **Have a bath.** Lock the door and luxuriate in a proper unrushed bath—scented candles, bubble bath, relaxing music—and breathe.
- **Read a book.** The older I get, the quicker I am to ditch books that aren't doing it for me. Because when you get the right book, even fifteen minutes of reading can transport you out of your head. (And seeing you reading for pleasure encourages children to read more too!) Or listen to an audiobook (perfect for commuting).

I'm sure your list is better than mine. Because when it comes to self-care, you know all of this already. You know you should be doing it. If you have fallen into the habit of putting yourself at the bottom of the to-do list, I give you permission to stop. In fact, I insist you stop. Looking after yourself will make you a better parent and your children will thank you for it. But more than that: you matter. Your well-being matters. It's not possible to have a happy family without a happy you. So carve out some pockets of time to do the things that make your spirit soar and your muscles relax and you will find your family life, and being a working parent, much more enjoyable.

ACTION POINTS

- Take a long hard look at all the tasks you are doing at home. How could you do less? Are there tasks you could drop, delegate, speed up, or postpone?
- Write down your big goals for family life (no more than three). Identify the goals that truly resonate with your dreams and values. How many of the tasks on your to-do list are making a *direct* contribution to those big goals?
- Make a list of quick-win self-care ideas that take between one minute and one hour. Keep the list somewhere handy for unexpected down time. Identify regular slots in your weekly schedule where you might be able to fit in a well-being moment.

12

Are You Doing More Than
Is Good for Your Children?

There is another reason why you need to look after yourself a little more and your children a little less: it is good for them. That might sound counterintuitive, but doing too much for your children gets in the way of them learning how to do things for themselves. And learning how to do things for themselves gives children a sense of mastery that is a vital component of good self-esteem. By doing too much, working parents not only risk grinding ourselves into a state of exhaustion, but we also deprive our children of opportunities to learn, succeed, and feel good about themselves.

Modern parents are laboring under a double whammy: we are working more and parenting more. For mothers, work has not replaced parenting, it has doubled the load. And modern fathers (who in previous generations might have taken a back seat in childcare) are now engaged in hands-on parenting on top of their day jobs. We are a generation of parents who believe that being a good parent really matters. We want to get it right. But it is easy to confuse "getting it right" with "doing it all."

In the past, being a good parent felt simpler. It meant giving basic things like love, shelter, food, and warmth, keeping kids clean, making sure they went to school, and telling them right from wrong. Being a good parent doesn't feel so simple these days—it seems to mean taking responsibility for every aspect of our children's lives. We worry about the impact of every little decision; we believe that being a good parent means doing everything we can to set our children up for success and happiness. We have written ourselves an impossible job description. There is so much to remember, so much to feel responsible for, and so much to do. It's hardly surprising that we are buckling under that mental load and that our brains are whirring with worries, tasks, and responsibilities.

Working parents constantly fret that we are not doing enough for our children. Actually, we are often doing too much. Wracked with guilt that we are not "there" enough, we dedicate our nonworking hours to supporting our children to succeed. We apply our superdeveloped efficiency thinking skills to planning and organizing every aspect of our children's lives, detecting and anticipating problems, vigilantly removing obstacles from their paths, and finding ways to rescue them from all potential discomforts (or feeling guilty if we can't). We don't want our children to miss out on anything, and we are quick to step in to prevent them experiencing failure or disappointment. We are risk-averse and interventionist project managers who give our children too little responsibility, allow them too little independence, and expect too little from them. Then, with no time left to recharge our batteries, we short circuit ourselves into relaxation through wine or TV shows.

Parental involvement is a great thing, but taking over and doing too much for our children risks not only stretching ourselves beyond what is humanly possible but also negatively impacting children's opportunities to develop good self-esteem. In order to develop a sense of self-worth and efficacy, they need to be allowed to do things for themselves, to make mistakes, and to apply the learning from their mistakes. Sometimes, when it comes to parenting, less really is more.

> **"Children with healthy self-esteem are much more likely to be resilient,
> be happy, be cooperative, and make friends easily."**

WHERE DOES SELF-ESTEEM COME FROM?

Self-esteem is the opinion we hold of our own skills and worth. It's not a real or objective fact, it's a subjective opinion we form based on interpretations of external evidence and of our own experiences. For example, two children could form a different interpretation of the same events, with different implications for their self-esteem. Take two players on the losing side in a football match. Objectively, they were both on the same team that lost the game and neither of them played well. One player might go away thinking, "That was a tough match. I played really badly. The rain made the ground slippery and the opposing team was bigger and better than we were. We were terrible defensively. We need to do some more practice on passing and defending set pieces so we don't let in so many goals next week." The other player might take away a totally different interpretation: "That was a tough match. I played really badly. If I hadn't messed up on that corner, we wouldn't have let in the first goal. And my passing was way off target. I'm terrible at football. I'm pretty sure they only pick me because there aren't enough players. I don't think I'll go to practice next week." Both of the players think they played badly, but one of them is interpreting the evidence in a way that opens up a window for change and progress, while the other is focusing on failure and drawing negative conclusions about their own self-worth. Same football match, different conclusions.

Good self-esteem is not about children having only positive experiences. It's about how children interpret those experiences. Children tend to feel good about themselves when they interpret their experiences in a way that makes them feel *accepted, competent,* and *effective.* Feeling *accepted* is about children feeling loved, wanted, and valued unconditionally for who they are. Feeling *competent* is about a sense of mastery; it's about children believing they can do things for themselves and that they are good at stuff. Feeling *effective* is that sense of agency that comes about when children see the connection between their efforts and the progress they make and believe that their actions make a difference. Good self-esteem comes from children understanding their experiences in ways that lead them to believe that they are lovable and valuable, that they are capable and skilled (in at least some areas), and that what they do makes a difference—that they have some control over outcomes.

Building children's self-esteem is not about making sure children have a failure-free life. It's not about telling them they are great at something when they are not. It's not about avoiding uncomfortable feelings or removing obstacles from their paths. It's not about pushing children to be as good as they can be. And it is not about dedicating our lives to meeting their needs. Building self-esteem is about loving our children unconditionally and providing opportunities for them to try, to succeed, and to fail and helping them interpret those experiences positively.

LET THEM TRY, LET THEM FAIL, LET THEM LEARN TO SUCCEED

If you are using the little bits of time you have around the edges of work to connect with your child and create meaningful moments, then you are well on the way to making them feel loved and accepted. Children feel valued when we spend time with them doing things we enjoy. Chat. Have fun. Chase that shiny wrapper. Be affectionate. Laugh—a lot! Enjoying their company sends a strong signal to children that they are accepted and acceptable just the way they are.

The temptation, however, is to take things one step further. To slip into the belief that loving children unconditionally means having no boundaries around what we do for them ("I'd do anything for my kids") and demonstrating the extent of our love by doing as much as we possibly can for them. Working parents are especially prone to this thinking trap because we so often carry guilt about not being at home "enough." We run around trying to make up for our absent hours by being Superparent when we get home, picking up abandoned yogurt cups (when they could do it themselves), organizing their school bags (when they could do it themselves), project-managing away all risk of failure, and rescuing them from every potentially negative situation (rather than helping them face challenges themselves and bounce back from their mistakes). We send our own stress levels sky-high by shouldering full responsibility for ensuring their lives run smoothly. And when something falls through the cracks, we rush to the rescue, juggling work meetings with manic text messages to arrange someone to take our daughter's forgotten lunchbox to school or adding extra weight to our already huge mental load by combing through our son's schoolwork every evening to avoid the possibility of him missing a piece of homework.

Sometimes this overparenting springs from a belief that the reason we are exhausting ourselves at work all day is to create a good life for our kids and that a good life doesn't involve failure or disappointments (it does). Sometimes adults use parenting as a crutch to shore up our own fragile self-esteem, trying as hard as we can to parent as well as we can so that we feel needed and worthy. Sometimes we just get stuck in perpetual work mode and see our children as a project that reflects on our own competence ("Look at me, I'm doing so much, so well! My child never forgets her gym clothes or homework and wears fabulous costumes on World Book Day! Look, I'm so involved! I remember it all and make sure it all gets done, ON TOP OF WORKING FULL TIME!").

And sometimes parents are just scared. We want to eliminate all risks from our children's lives because the thought of them feeling pain is just too awful to bear.

But the problem with doing too much for our children is that though it might bolster parents' self-worth, it does the opposite for children's self-esteem. Having someone else who remembers things for them deprives children of precious opportunities to build their own self-esteem by becoming capable and independent. Having someone who always makes sure they don't make mistakes (and who steps in and makes it all better when they do) renders children powerless rather than making them feel effective. Overparenting sends children the message "I think you can't do it, that's why I'm doing it," undermining their sense of competence. Rather than mistakes being seen as an inevitable component of learning (because mistakes teach us how to do something better), overparenting sends the signal that failure is to be avoided at all costs, engendering a fear of failure that can push children to perfectionism or stop them from trying altogether. By removing obstacles from children's paths to spare them uncomfortable feelings, we are really saying, "I don't think you are strong enough to cope." When parents underestimate children's capacity to get things right, children learn to underestimate themselves too.

Every single skill children master, every tiny obstacle they overcome, contributes to building their self-esteem. Whether it's the tricky-shaped play brick that a toddler finally manages to post through the right hole or a difficult friendship group that a tween learns to navigate, good self-esteem is built on children believing "I can do it if I keep trying." Children's sense of achievement doesn't just come from those successes in sports, music, or school that parents love to post on social media; the little everyday things matter just as much. When children succeed in doing something, anything, they have an opportunity to feel proud of themselves. Experiencing success by putting on your own pants is a self-esteem-building moment.

So teach your child to be independent—expect them to get dressed by themselves, tidy their toys, pack their own school bags, clean up after dinner, load the dishwasher, and contribute to household chores. These little daily triumphs help children feel competent (and mean that you have less to do!). And the more children are doing for themselves, the less you have to do and the lighter the mental load you have to carry.

> **"Being treated as someone who has a contribution to make to the family, rather than as a little prince or princess, builds a sense of self-worth."**

Whenever possible, challenge yourself to get out of your children's way and let them try. By stepping back and letting children do it, we send the signal "You've got this." Even if they don't succeed, we can help them interpret their experiences positively by drawing attention to the progress they are making ("You nearly did it! That was better than last time! You tried really hard!"). By acknowledging their efforts and their progress, we model a positive interpretation of events for them to internalize.

THINKING POINT

Benchmark your practical expectations of your child against the expectations of their childcarer or school. When it comes to helping out—mealtimes, clearing up, changing clothes, responsibility for personal possessions and personal hygiene—are they expected to have the same level of independence at home as they do at school/in childcare?

However, remember, attention is a superpower, so use it wisely and don't be scattergun with your praise. Constantly telling your child they are wonderful, amazing, and "The Best" quickly loses its effectiveness. Overblown praise can actually inhibit children's learning:

Parent: You're so good at math!

Child's conclusion: *I am already good enough, I don't need to try.*

Overblown praise can destroy trust:

Parent: You're the best mathematician ever.

Child's conclusion: *I don't believe your opinion of me as it clearly isn't based on reality.*

And it can undermine self-esteem by creating a fear of failure:

Parent: I am so proud of you for doing so well in math.

Child's conclusion: *I always need to do things perfectly in order to be approved of.*

Praise helps build self-esteem best when it is specific and believable and when it helps children interpret their failures positively. If your daughter performs really badly in a music recital and you tell her she played brilliantly, it won't help her self-esteem. Focus on real achievements and on effort. If she comes off the stage and says, "I'm terrible at violin," don't say, "No, you're not." It won't help her. Model a positive interpretation by saying, "*That was a tough piece to play. I saw you lost your place. Well done for not giving up and for playing all the way to the end, that was really impressive.* Hopefully, it won't be such a tough piece next time." And show her how to move on from those moments.

In the workplace, we are surrounded by a culture in which failure is bad. Failure means lost profits, no bonus, and, ultimately, no job. But children need a family culture in which failure and getting things wrong is good; in which failure is an opportunity for learning ("I got it wrong—yippee! Now I know not to do that again!"). Interpreted positively, mistakes are one of those natural child development pull factors that mean parents can do less pushing.

Push or Pull Factors

Rather than shouldering the full brunt of responsibility for every aspect of our children's lives, parenting using pull factors involves handing over responsibility by positioning children as active and accountable participants in their own futures. Pull factors are about maximizing children's self-led learning. Encouraging children to set their own goals, evaluate their own achievements, and adjust their own actions are the prime ways to engage pull factors. Pull factors are a great way to help build confidence and self-esteem and they are especially useful for children who lack self-belief or who are struggling with a task.

Take reading as an example. Your daughter comes home from school with a reading book. Her educational target is to move up a reading level by the end of the term. But she doesn't enjoy reading, so progress is slow. She doesn't think she's very good at reading (and the fact that she is a level behind her classmates confirms that). As a parent eager to support learning, one response would be to push: "You've got to read this whole book tonight so you can make as much progress as possible to catch up." But when every mistake already makes her feel like a failure, that's not an enticing prospect, so the chances of tears, opting out, or pushback are high.

A pull factor approach might be to say, "OK, you've got a new book. How many pages do you think you can read tonight?" If she is a reluctant reader or unconfident, she will probably go for a really low target: "Just one page." Don't push, just say, "OK, give it a go." If she has set a low target, she will probably achieve it easily. But in achieving it, she will experience a glimmer of competence. Then you can encourage her to self-evaluate: "How was that? Was it easy or hard to read that much? How much more do you think you can read tomorrow?" If she has experienced success, she is quite likely to up her target (if not the very next time, then soon). But more importantly, she will feel more in control and good about herself. After a few weeks of this self-led process, she will be reading the whole book the first time, whereas if she had failed at your whole-book stretch target on the first day, that failure would have led her to negative conclusions ("Reading is really hard/boring/I'm terrible at it"), confirming her sense of incompetence and making her less likely to try again.

If, on the other hand, she sets a ridiculously high target, don't argue with her. Start on the journey and see how far she gets (she might surprise you!).

And if she can't reach it, ask her whether maybe her goal was too big for one day and help her to break it down into smaller daily steps.

When parents encourage children to set their own goals, evaluate, learn from their mistakes, and adjust their course, children experience a true sense of "I can do this." Parenting using pull factors is all about asking questions. So when your child shows you a drawing, rather than heaping on the overblown praise, ask them what they think of it ("I really like the colors you've used. Are you pleased with it? Which bit do you like best?"). Similarly, if they tell you what marks they got at school, ask, "How do you feel about that score?" Key questions to generate pull factors include:

- Are you pleased with the result?
- What did you do well?
- What could you have done better?
- Did you do anything differently this time?
- What will you do differently next time?

Parenting using pull factors means parents doing less work (both mentally and physically) and putting the onus on children to be more active in managing their own lives. For a toddler that might just mean getting themselves dressed (at least the easy parts!). For a preschooler, it might mean keeping their toys tidy. And for a primary school child, it might mean being in charge of their own school bag.

"But what if she won't take responsibility and just keeps forgetting her lunchbox? I can't let her go hungry!" Using pull factors and allowing children to make mistakes doesn't mean that we throw up our hands and stop teaching them. It means that we help them learn from mistakes rather than always rescuing them. If your daughter keeps forgetting her lunch and you are worried about her going hungry, the questions you should be asking are: "What can you do to help yourself remember?" and "What can you do if you forget?" (Not "What can I do to make sure you don't forget?") Help her to come up with aide memoires and backup plans, yes, but put the onus on her to do the remembering.

If you keep doing the remembering and the organizing, your children won't learn to take responsibility or find ways to do it for themselves. If you always insist on adding everything to your own to-do list, it's going to take a very long time for your child to step up and take responsibility for themselves. And in the meantime, your frenzied cycle of planning, organizing, and remembering everything makes it much harder to switch into your loving, curious, playful parent mode and creates a debilitating mental load that inevitably fuels resentment ("Why am I doing all this? For goodness sake how hard is it to remember your lunch?"). It's a cycle of blame, resentment, and learned incompetence.

The same lack of frontal lobe brain development that means children don't do efficiency thinking also makes them very likely to forget things. Very infuriating for hyperorganized parents! Encourage your daughter to put a checklist on the fridge (a "Don't forget to do these things after breakfast" checklist) or by the front door (a "List of equipment needed for school" checklist). Or a photo showing everything that should be in their school bag if words don't do it for them. I taught my son to tuck notes into his school shoes the night before if there was something he needed to remember to take—sometimes he forgot to write the note and he forgot to take the equipment, but slowly he learned that the note was a good idea. Corkboards or whiteboards in bedrooms are great places to put important papers that mustn't be lost and to write themselves reminder messages. Encourage older children to write an equipment list on their whiteboard and prompt them to check their board if you think they have forgotten something. (And if they say that they have everything but you know their reading book is still on the sofa, do no more than prompt "Are you sure?" The point is for them to learn to remember by themselves.) Praise them if they remember to take all their equipment and, if they forget, don't run to the rescue—let them problem solve it for themselves. And when you get home just say, "Hey ho. What are you going to do differently to make sure you remember tomorrow?"

THINKING POINT

Think back to your own childhood. At what age did you go to the park without an adult? Or to the shops? When did you learn to change a lightbulb or a plug? What jobs did you have to do around the house? What happened if you forgot to take something to school (like your house key, lunch, or reading book)?

THE PRINCIPLE OF MINIMAL ASSISTANCE

If you want to reduce your mental and physical load and encourage your child's independence, the principle of minimal assistance is another really useful motto to parent by. It's a neat way of ensuring that your child gets as little or as much help as they need in order to learn a new skill. And when children learn to do things for themselves, you will have one less thing to fit into your busy schedule!

On the scale of parental assistance, doing a task *for* your child counts as maximum assistance. Leaving them to get on with it unaided is zero assistance (or full independence). So far, so simple.

The difficulties often arise when faced with a task that your child hasn't yet mastered or a complex task that has lots of stages, like washing your own hair, for example. If your daughter can't yet wash her own hair, the temptation is to just keep doing it for her. It's quicker that way. And you know that if you just leave her to get on with it, there's a good chance of an unsuccessful (or uncomfortable) outcome—shampoo in her eyes, knots and tangles, water on the floor, or still-dirty hair, to name a few! But as long as you keep taking over and doing it for her, she will never learn to do it by herself. And she will miss out on a chance to master a new skill and have that feel-good competence boost to her self-esteem. This is where the principle of minimal assistance comes in.

The principle of minimal assistance is a way to help children become independent by giving them only the amount of help they actually need in order to master a new or complex task. Here's how it works.

Step 1: Break the task down into steps.

Washing your own hair involves doing certain things in a certain order. First you need to wet your hair, then put the right amount of shampoo into your hand, and then transfer the shampoo onto your head and rub it in (avoiding sensitive eyes). The shampoo then needs to be rinsed out and the wet hair towel-dried and combed. That's a lot to learn. So it's best to focus on just one step at a time. When a task has lots of stages, take the learning in stages.

Step 2: Check what they already know.

Once you have broken it down into steps in your mind, rather than jumping in and telling your daughter how to do each step, first check what she already knows. Ask, "*What's the first step?*" If she answers correctly, great! You can move straight on to practicing that first step. If the answer is wrong ("*I need to put the shampoo on my hand*") then you can tell her the first step: "*That comes later. First you need to put water on your hair.*" By checking what she already knows, you start the learning at the right place and the principle of minimal assistance is in action.

Step 3: Let them have a go.

Once your child is clear on what the first step is, suggest that she has a go at it. Say, "*Why don't you try that by yourself?*" then step back and let her have a go. If she manages it, great! She has already gotten through the first step and you haven't had to do anything at all—that's the principle of minimal assistance. If she is reluctant to try alone, or struggles to do it, then step in and help her by doing it together. Show her how to get her own hair wet.

Step 4: Repeat.

For a younger child, or a child who is going to need a bit more practice, you might want to leave it there. Repeat the same sequence the next bath time, until she has that first step nailed. (Or if that first step is just too hard, maybe skip on to the next step and see if she can do that one by herself.) If she is on a roll and has the first step mastered, move on to the second step and then the third step, repeating the same pattern each time. Remember to ask first, don't just jump in and help: "*What's the next thing you have to do?*" If she knows the next step, suggest she gives it a go. Only assist if you are really needed (sit on your hands if you have to!). And before you know it, she'll be doing the whole thing by herself.

> **"Teaching any independent new skill means accepting that your child may not do it exactly the same way you do it. And they may not do it as well as you."**

Remember, it's the process here that is important. Your child feeling a growing sense of competence through a happy trial-and-error process is the real point. Get the process right and the outcome (her being more independent, you having less to do) will follow. And don't micromanage. If you tell her she has done it wrong or just take over, the message you are giving is "You're no good at this." And if children hear that message often enough, what they understand is "I'm not good enough." Positive results can spring from failure as long as the message children take away is "I can work out a way to get better at this." Start by doing a little less and before you know it, you'll be doing a lot less. And your brain will be a lot less full of the grinding minutiae that can so easily distract us from actually enjoying our family time and our children.

ACTION POINT

- Let your child(ren) make lunch/dinner this weekend. Let them plan the menu themselves and work out what they need and how to do it. With younger children you will have to set limits around using the oven or sharp knives but, as much as possible, let them do everything themselves. If a cooked dinner is too big a challenge, propose an indoor picnic.

13

Riding the Rollercoaster
of Emotions

It isn't just the sheer amount of stuff that working parents have to squeeze into our days that makes the work/parent switch so challenging. There is the little matter of children's emotions too—and their knock-on effect on our emotions. Children are unpredictable and volatile creatures. They are prone to outbursts, meltdowns, and flare-ups and can go from zero to ten out of the blue, seemingly at the most trivial of triggers. Controlling your own emotions in the face of a child who has not yet mastered theirs is a big ask when you are already running on empty at the end of a working day.

It's easy to dismiss children's emotions as ridiculous or overblown. Their intensity often strikes adults as misplaced ("All that fuss just because I used the wrong colored cup?!"). But children's big feelings can quickly start to dominate family life and they are usually at the root of children's most antisocial and up-setting behavior—whether that's crying, shouting, or lashing out. And when those big feelings are directed at you—their devoted parent who is working your fingers to the bone to make everything right for them—it's hard not to jump on to their emotional bandwagon and join in. To feel angry too. Or upset. Or like a failure as a parent.

We all love our children deeply and we desperately want to protect them from uncomfortable or painful feelings. But the truth is, we can't. We cannot arrange our children's lives to avoid every tear and tantrum or to sidestep every frustration or hurt. Believing that it's our job to cushion every potential setback and rescue them from every emotional trough is an efficiency thinking trap that simply sets up working parents for a whole heap of exhaustion, guilt, and failure. Because it is an impossible task. You could run through your day like an Olympian carrying a world record–breaking mental load and still not manage to protect your child from life's difficult ups and downs. All you will succeed in doing is grinding yourself into a state of exhaustion in which you are more (not less) likely to react emotionally to parenting's inevitable knocks.

> **"We cannot wrap our children in cotton wool and protect them from every emotional challenge. And if we could, we would be doing them no favors."**

The principle of minimal assistance that we saw in the previous chapter applies equally to children's emotional world as to practical tasks. It's not a parent's job to take away children's emotions or to solve every problem; it's our job to help them learn to manage their emotions for themselves. What children really need from us is to help them learn the emotional skills and resilience to manage their own rollercoaster, so that they can face life's challenges positively, recover from life's unavoidable hurts, and bounce back from their difficult feelings quickly.

When it comes to emotions, switching out of work mode and into parent mode means ditching that urge to run around meeting every goal, eliminating every risk, fixing every problem, and cushioning every knock and instead learning to listen to our children's emotions and to be still in their difficult moments. It requires parents to do something less active but fundamentally more therapeutic—being present in a way that helps our children feel safe and understood and that allows them to ride out their emotions and find their own equanimity. And for that, we need to hold our own feelings in check, manage our emotional boundaries well, and rise to children's big moments with some truly empathetic listening.

THAT'S NOT MY JUICE!

Let's be honest. Children's off-the-scale emotional outbursts can elicit a variety of responses in tired parents. Sometimes we find them funny, sometimes utterly infuriating, and sometimes deeply upsetting. But why do young children go off the emotional deep end quite so much?

The first thing to remember is that children simply don't have much emotional life experience behind them. By the time we become parents, most adults have experienced our fair share of emotions—good ones, bad ones, highs and lows. We are familiar with the pattern of emotions and have developed a few strategies (healthy or otherwise) to manage our feelings. We have learned to walk away when we are enraged and to breathe deeply when we are nervous. When we are knocked over by sadness, even in the depth of that emotion, we know from experience that the sadness will eventually pass. And we have a few tried-and-tested ways to pick ourselves back up again.

It's easy to forget that children don't have that knowledge. Children are not born understanding what an emotion is. Emotions are intense and physical sensations that can completely take over our thoughts and actions. Imagine what it must be like to be a very young child having a big feeling like anger welling up inside you and having no words to describe it. Not knowing what that feeling is or how to make it go away. Feeling possessed by an unknown surge and not knowing how big it is going to get, whether it will ever stop, or whether it will just get bigger and bigger until it blows you apart. That's a frightening place to be. A big emotion can literally pick a child up off the floor and throw them to the ground. It takes the whole of their childhood for children to learn what emotions are, how to express them, and what they can do to gain some control over them.

It also takes some pretty advanced brain development. Children can appear to go off the deep end over tiny triggers because they live in a fundamentally different world from adults. The physical properties of the universe that parents take for granted are simply beyond a young child's cognitive development. The fact that half-melted ice pops can't be put back on their sticks, that teddies absorb water and take time to dry, or that if you splash in a puddle in wellies your feet can still get wet—these things are not givens in a young child's world. When they happen, they are a genuine surprise! Imagine living in a world in which unrectifiable things happened frequently and unpredictably—you'd probably get knocked off your emotional balance a few times a day too!

From a parent's perspective, this lack of understanding often comes across as stubbornness. Take the classic red cup/blue cup "That's not my juice!" meltdown. As adults, we know that juice is the same no matter which cup it is in. So when a thirsty young child goes into full-on meltdown because we have put their juice in the wrong cup, to us that is unreasonable and ridiculous behavior and their reaction is in no way justified by the situation. However, from the young child's perspective, the situation looks completely different. Young children do not believe that the same juice is the same juice no matter which cup it is in. The idea that a liquid stays the same but adopts the shape of its container is a sophisticated scientific principle (called "conservation"), and children don't develop the cognitive agility to understand that principle until they are about six or seven years old. If you pour a drink from a short, wide cup to a tall, thin cup in front of a four-year-old, they will likely believe that there is "more" drink in the tall cup despite having watched you pour the same drink from one cup to another. Young children can't compute that different shapes and sizes of containers hold the same amount of liquid. In their heads, the juice in the red cup really is different from the juice in the blue cup because it looks different. It's a completely different juice! It will take a few more years of splashing in the bath and repetitively pouring water from one container to another for your preschooler to grasp the abstract concepts of volume, size, and transferability. To us, it looks like they are making a lot of fuss about a cup. But to them, you are trying to make them drink the completely wrong juice. It's a very different perspective.

Without that well-developed prefrontal cortex that enables adults to weigh up risks and make accurate predictions (and that drives working parents' efficiency thinking), children are wonderfully and wholeheartedly invested in their moment-to-moment activities. But they are also very vulnerable to unpredictable upset and uncontainable disappointment. Play really matters to children; they are driven to play from a strong internal urge. Play is how they meet their developmental needs—whether that is learning spatial skills by rotating an object to post it through a hole (for a toddler) or learning how to be liked and fit in socially (for a ten-year-old). So when your toddler can't get that brick to fit through the hole or your tween is not invited to a party, it really affects them. And their corresponding emotions, although they might seem ridiculous or "wrong" to us, are huge and genuine. My seven-year-old was once truly and utterly heartbroken when he failed to win a giant Sponge-Bob SquarePants at a fairground stall. He wanted it so badly. He cried for two hours (literally!) then insisted on going back the next day to try again. And when, the next day, he also failed to knock off those three cans with his ball (despite being warned that the chances were infinitesimally small and that the game was probably rigged anyway), his heart broke all over again. To me, it was just a big cuddly toy. To him, it was the thing that mattered most in the whole wide world.

HELPING CHILDREN MANAGE THEIR EMOTIONS

Now, the temptation for us solution-focused efficiency thinking adults, of course, is to try to erase children's hurts and ease their pain by bribing the stallholder to give you that cuddly SpongeBob (I tried—he wouldn't!) or by phoning the birthday girl's mom to get an invitation to the party. But we are doing our children no favors that way. Because it is through experiencing those momentous feelings and finding a route back to equilibrium that children develop emotional resilience. Children learn through these challenging experiences how to regulate their emotions and dial down their hair-trigger reactions. And they can't learn to be emotionally resilient if mom or dad always rescues them.

Emotional resilience is a bit like being a foam ball rather than an egg. Drop an egg on the floor and it will go splat, whereas the ball will bounce up again. The ball might get a little dented, but it isn't broken. Being emotionally re-silient doesn't mean that your children won't have big or difficult feelings but that they can recognize those feelings for what they are and have mechanisms for riding them out and helping them pass. It isn't a parent's job to take away children's big emotional waves; it's our job to teach them how to surf.

At work, we are used to having our responsibilities clearly defined. We know which inputs and outputs are expected from us. And in the best organizations, we have a clear sense of the overall outcomes we and our colleagues are work-ing toward. But at home, things are fuzzier. It's easy to confuse "I want my child to be happy" with "It's my job to keep my child happy" and to take on responsibility (and blame) for every tear and tantrum. But it's not your job to keep your child happy. Yes, it is your job to try to set them up with the condi-tions and skills likely to lead to happiness. But it is not your job to maintain your child's equanimity for them. Your job is to help them learn to do that for themselves.

Rather than jumping in to fix things, the best way parents can help children manage their emotions is simply by acknowledging their emotion and giving it a name. When your child is being emotional, stop, listen, and name the emotion you see: "I can see you are really disappointed that you didn't win SpongeBob. I know you wanted it so much. It doesn't feel fair because you tried so hard." It won't change the situation, but by giving a word to that big feeling (and a cuddle), the feeling becomes less overwhelming. If it has a name, then it can be known, discussed, and recovered from.

"But what if their emotion is leading them to attack their little sister with a toy hammer?!" True, one of the most challenging things about young children is that they often express feelings like anger in unacceptable ways—by shout-ing, hitting, lashing out, or having a loud embarrassing tantrum in the middle of the gift shop. No child ever approached a parent and said calmly, "Mommy, I am feeling enraged!" They show it in their actions, and these actions can look pretty barbaric to adult eyes. Children are not born knowing how to control their impulses (toddlers can't even control their own body parts, for goodness sake, let alone their thoughts!). But just because children often express their emotions in socially wrong ways doesn't mean that their emotions are wrong. Our feelings are our feelings. We can't help which feelings we have, but we can learn to express those feelings in appropriate ways. If your child's anger is leading them to behave unacceptably, name the emotion you can see but also guide them toward an appropriate way to manage or express that feeling. For example, "I can see you are angry because your sister broke your toy. But it is not OK to throw things. Find a safe place to calm down until you can speak quietly to tell me what happened."

> **"Naming children's emotions helps them feel that their emotion has been heard."**

Emotions are attention seeking: they desperately want to be noticed. And if they aren't given recognition, they keep trying different ways to get into the light. When children don't feel that their emotion has been recognized, they are much more likely to escalate their behavior in a bid to communicate that unheard emotion—crying turns into shouting, and shouting turns into hitting. Children's emotional outbursts often escalate when parents just focus on their behavior and fail to acknowledge their emotional root. In contrast, when adults stay calm and children feel understood, their heightened emotions can start to subside.

BIG MOMENT LISTENING

When big stuff happens at work, we jump into action. There are emergency meetings, action plans, press releases—a whirlwind of activity. But when really big stuff happens in children's worlds and there are truly painful emotions involved, the very last thing they need from parents is a whirlwind, which is difficult because for many parents, these are exactly the moments when it is hardest to stay calm and not get snatched up by the emotional rollercoaster.

I know it's hard to think about it, but difficult things will happen in your child's life. Whether it's a loss in the family, bullying, or just the inevitable disappointments of not succeeding at something they hold dear, all our children will face challenges and they will feel hurt. Most of us aspire to a relationship with our children in which they will talk to us when there is something wrong. Yet the main reason children cite for not telling their parents about something important is fear that we will overreact. And they're right. Too often parents respond to children's big situations by reacting rather than listening. We try to get rid of their pain as quickly as possible by soothing or reasoning, or we get consumed by the lion/ess rising inside us and leap to defend our cub, dashing off an unwise email to the head teacher or trying to make things right. Or we blame our children for having got themselves into a difficult situation, telling them what they should or shouldn't have done, and what they should or shouldn't feel.

What children really need is for parents to bring calm (not work stress, battle stations, or our own emotional baggage) to their big moments. And to do that, we need to be switched fully into parent mode and rise to their big moments with some empathetic listening.

Empathetic listening is parent mode in its purest form. It is the polar opposite of the quick-thinking task-focused efficiency thinking that serves us so well at work. Empathetic listening involves doing less rather than more. Being still rather than acting. Bringing your full attention to the present moment and suspending your judgments and reactions. Listening to your child and signaling that you have heard what they have said. It means allowing space for your child to find their words, reflecting back to them what you hear, and acknowledging that how they are feeling is valid (even if you disagree with it). Just by being patient and allowing the full problem to come out, this "big moment listening" reassures your child that, no matter how big, this challenge won't make mom or dad panic, so it must be manageable (*even though I have never faced it before*). That this is a feeling that mom or dad can understand, so it must be survivable (*even though I have never felt it before*). And that there might be things that I can do that will make a difference (*even if I have never tried them before*).

So when those big moments come along and your child is distressed or talking to you about something difficult, be quiet. Don't offer advice. Zip your mouth shut and just listen. When there is a pause, briefly summarize back to them what you have heard and what feelings you have identified:

> Parent: *It sounds like you're really disappointed because you didn't get chosen to be in the play. That's tough, I know how much you were hoping to be in it.*

Having someone present with them who recognizes how they feel but isn't in that emotion themselves makes children's emotions feel more bearable, more recoverable from, that it's OK to have that feeling, and that there will be an end to it. Naming your child's emotion and summarizing back to them what you have heard will help them feel understood. And if you haven't understood correctly, it gives your child a chance to keep trying to explain until you do understand:

> Child: I'm not disappointed, I'm ashamed. I was so bad in the audition. I can't show my face there again, I'm not going next week. Everyone else got picked.

The goal of big moment listening is simply to make children feel understood. It is not about influencing your child or showing them the way forward, it is first and foremost about signaling that you see where they are at right now. Empathetic listening conveys acceptance, that the emotion your child is experiencing is real and valid. It creates a space in which children feel safe to tell you anything, no matter how difficult, because they trust that they will be supported, not criticized.

> Parent: That's a really difficult feeling. It's hard when something important goes wrong and people are watching us.

Even if your child's big communication strikes you as misplaced or out of proportion, try not to belittle their feelings. Don't use the words "should" or "shouldn't" (*"You shouldn't feel bad, you were in the play last term. And I bet you weren't the only one who had a bad day"*). Being told you are having the wrong emotion is exactly the opposite of feeling understood! Your child feels the way they feel. Your job is to connect with their actual feeling and help them find a way to manage it positively. The fact that you (or another child) might feel differently in the same situation is just not relevant.

Resist the pull of your solution-focused thinking. Empathetic listening is about not doing anything, it is just about being there alongside your child. Once the initial emotion seems to have calmed, guide them toward their own solution by coaching them through the problem-solving steps: *"What are your options now?"* And help them think through the consequences of their ideas: "What might happen if you did that?" You don't have to agree with their choices, you are entitled to an opinion about what they should/shouldn't do (just not about what they should/shouldn't feel—that's not something they can control).

> Parent: In my opinion, being part of the backstage crew would be a better idea than walking away. I know you are disappointed now but it would probably be fun. It's your decision. Why don't you think about it for a while before you decide?

Of course, not every problem has a solution. Family is not like work. Sometimes there is nothing to be done and the best we can do is to help children find positive ways to cope by asking questions like, "What could you do to cheer yourself up?" or "Is there something you could think about that would make you feel happier?" But if we can bring calm rather than activity to children's big moments, although we won't fix anything, our children will learn emotional skills and coping mechanisms that can help them bounce back from difficult moments for the rest of their lives.

WHEN THEIR EMOTIONS TRIGGER YOUR EMOTIONS

Bringing calm to children's emotional chaos presupposes, of course, that the adults involved are at least a little bit in control of our own emotional rollercoaster. Which is not a given. Becoming a parent brings with it a host of overwhelming feelings, both harrowing and beautiful: the surge of pure love when you watch your child sleeping, the tears of joy when they stand on stage and mumble their lines in their first school play, the rush of sheer fear when they aren't in the place where you expected them to be, the roar of anger that shakes us like a primeval lion/ess when something threatens our child. Being a parent connects us to a place deep inside us full of need, fear, hope, and hurt. We care so much about our children and feel so responsible for them, we are truly vulnerable. It's not an easy ride.

Emotional resilience is something parents need too. And working parents need extra helpings of it. One of the best ways you can boost resilience is by maintaining strong connections (with people other than our children!). Whether that's friends or family, spend time with people who make you feel likable and valued and that, maybe, you aren't making such a terrible hash of everything after all. Or with people who will just listen when you really do need to tell them what a mess everything feels. Being a part of something that has greater meaning (whether that's a sports team, community, cause, or faith) has been shown to be a huge source of resilience and an essential antidote to that lack of perspective that comes when we feel isolated. And we can all top up our own emotional resources by remembering to prioritize simple everyday actions that improve physical well-being and foster good mental health, such as having a healthy diet, regularly exercising, and getting enough sleep.

But if you find, despite your best efforts, that your own emotional rollercoaster is particularly volatile or that your child's daily ups and downs are setting off a parental maelstrom in response, it's worth stepping back and asking yourself why. What is it about your child's emotional world that so directly triggers yours? By interrogating the underlying beliefs that are triggering our big emotional responses, we can sometimes talk back to those thoughts, get a little distance on those reactions, and plot an alternative route.

THINKING POINT

What coping skills do you use to manage your own big emotions? Do you use a relaxation strategy like taking deep breaths? Or distract yourself by trying to think about something else? Do you use positive self-talk to tell yourself it will all be OK? Or maybe you put all of those together by going for a walk? What coping skills does your child use to calm their big emotions?

There are lots of reasons why parents' emotional responses might get out of hand. Sometimes it stems from an anxiety to get parenting right. Working parents are especially vulnerable to this when we are worried that we are not "there" enough. Being a working parent feels a lot like trying to run a very long race carrying a very heavy sack. Every day we pick up information about another worry that needs to be put in our sack, another thing we must or mustn't do with/for our children. And when those fears and worries get on top of us, we can tip into overcaring about every detail. We get stuck in the minutiae of our children's lives and lose sight of the bigger picture ("If I can just keep a firm grip on every detail and make everything right, then I must be doing all right as a parent"). We overthink every risk and rush around to cushion, arrange, and mitigate at every pass. We do too much and miss the point. Everything matters. And when everything matters, everything has the power to tip us over the edge when it goes wrong.

Or perhaps your emotional reactivity springs from another classic efficiency thinking trap, focusing on the performance indicators. Could your volatile parental emotions be because you care just a little too much about your child's achievements? If you are a high-achieving career-driven parent, there is a good chance that you locate a fair portion of your self-esteem in success. And when that's the case, it's easy to place too much value in the badges of our children's academic/sporting/musical successes too. Or maybe you have fallen into the trap of believing that your child's outcomes validate your worth as a parent? Because if that's the case, when anything threatens your child's success, your panic button is going to get pushed and you are going to take every knockback very personally.

These are hard questions. And maybe you can find a little bit of yourself in all of those explanations. But as long as you are using (even a tiny bit) feeling like a good parent as an emotional prop for feeling like a good person, you will only be a hair's breadth away from feeling like a bad person because you think you are being a bad parent.

Riding the parenting rollercoaster means accepting the fundamental but uncomfortable truth that your child is an autonomous individual over whom you have some influence but not control. Children are not the sum total of our efforts. And we are not the sum total of our children's successes. You can't keep adding more and more to your parenting load. You will just run yourself into the ground or things will start falling apart (and they might be important things). The only sure way to succeed in the working parent race is to lighten the load by focusing on what matters and what's possible. And that means accepting that your parenting is not the be-all and end-all of your child's life—you are only one part of their picture.

And that might just be your most liberating thought yet.

ACTION POINT

- Help young children develop emotional literacy by talking about people's feelings and intentions. When you are reading a book together, ask how the character might be feeling or why they might be acting in a particular way. Encourage them to think about how they would feel/act in the same circumstances.

14

Step Away from the Blame Game

I would love to promise you that if you do everything I've said in this book, you and your child will be 100 percent happy. Or to hand you a secret recipe ("Ta da!") containing the ideal number of hours to work for a perfect work/life balance. Or say that as long as you get home by 7:00 p.m. at least three nights a week, everything will be hunky-dory. But I can't say that. Because there is no universal magic formula for being a parent that will absolutely guarantee your child's success and happiness (and don't believe anyone who tells you they've found one). Children's lives are determined by more than just their parenting. And difficult things can still happen to children who have had great parenting.

That's not to say that positive parenting strategies can't be learned (they can). Or that good parenting doesn't matter (it does). But to believe that all our children's outcomes are directly under our control is a false assumption. And it creates a huge amount of pressure to get everything right: "If I can just do it *all* right, do *everything* I've read in the parenting manuals and cover *all* the bases, then I will make my child happy and successful." It's not that simple. And if we fall into the trap of thinking that how our children turn out is all about us, we line ourselves up for blame and guilt whenever things don't go perfectly—whether that's a toddler who bites another tot, a child who lags behind in reading, or a tween who says she hates herself—"It must be my fault."

At work, we are used to controlling the controllables, measuring our success, and working to a plan. We set targets, track key performance indicators, and hold annual appraisals. But parenting is fundamentally different from work. Nobody has given us the plan and there is no handbook on how our specific child works. We can't plot our parenting performance on a graph. Parenting is more like being a medieval farmer than a modern-day worker—we can care for our plants, give them what they need to thrive, and be mindful of the changing seasons, but ultimately we can't control the clouds. And the weather will have a big say in how our crops grow.

If we go looking for certainty, then parenting is deeply uncomfortable. Our children are the people we care about most in the world and yet we can never really be sure exactly what the right thing to do for them at any given moment is. Parenting is a series of difficult judgment calls, not a science. Being able to find happiness in the midst of that uncertainty means stepping away from the blame game and accepting that we are only part of our child's picture.

WE ARE NOT AS IMPORTANT AS WE THINK WE ARE

Modern parents love to think that we're very important, that we are the deciding factor in our children's lives. When Sammy gets the "Player of the Week" award, we post it on social media for all our friends to see: "Look! Look how well my child is doing! Aren't I doing well at parenting!" When my son was made deputy head boy at his school, all my friends told me what a credit he was to me. And when his brother dropped out of college, none of them explicitly told me I was to blame, but it was impossible for me not to think it. Because giving parents the credit for children's success is just the flipside of blaming the parents (or yourself) when things go wrong.

This "take the credit"/"blame the parents" thinking assumes that parents are far more important than we really are. It supposes that (a) we can freely choose how we parent and (b) our kids are totally shaped by their environment. It tends to forget that there is a child in the mix with their own unique set of variables.

Don't get me wrong, I haven't been conning you—there is definitely consistent evidence from quality research that certain parenting styles and strategies are associated with good outcomes for children. But, equally, there is clear evidence that the genetic factors that predispose us to certain personality traits are also influential on children's long-term well-being. Both nature and nurture are at play in children's development. And once a mate has been chosen and the genetic deed has been done, parenting is only one part of the jigsaw.

Indeed, parenting itself is not a freely chosen activity. It's not something that parents truly control. How we parent is fundamentally affected by our personal history, by our environment, and by our child's responses. Parenting is not a one-way process in which parents "do" parenting and children passively receive it. Your child's innate personality has a direct impact on your parenting style. It's a two-way relationship. Rather than parenting being something that parents "do," it is more accurate to understand parenting as a transactional and mutually influential dynamic on which both parents and children exert influence. Children who are more agreeable and conscientious, for example, tend to have parents who parent with greater warmth. And children with lower agreeableness have parents who parent with more stress. (Easy-tempered, hard-working children are much easier to parent!) Our child's genetically determined temperament feeds into the way we parent, and the way we parent then affects how our child behaves and how they express their temperament.

Believing that we are the be-all and end-all of our children's futures (seeking all the credit, assuming all the blame) does not lead to good parenting decisions. It just makes us try too hard, run away, or find unhelpful ways of managing the guilt and worry of feeling like we're getting it wrong. Guilt and blame are huge psychological weights to carry. To feel happy as a working parent, you have to accept that doubt, failure, and uncertainty are integral to parenting. And you are not in control of the outcomes. We have to forgive ourselves (and our children) for not being perfect and learn to live with uncertainty and imperfection without it knocking us off course.

GOOD ENOUGH IS GOOD ENOUGH

There is no such thing as a perfect parent, and aiming to be one is bad for parents and bad for children. Children need their parents to be just good enough—no more, no less. Good enough is good enough. You and I both know that despite having read this book and promised yourself wholeheartedly that you'll be a calm, consistent, and playful parent from now on, you will still forget that in the heat of the moment. One day next week, you'll find yourself reasoning, shouting, or forgetting to listen and slipping back into efficiency thinking habits. And you'll be tempted to throw your hands in the air and give up, concluding that either you (or the book) are just terrible.

It isn't possible to do everything right in parenting. Brilliant parenting can never inoculate children against bad outcomes. Life just isn't that simple and nor are children. Parenting is a numbers game: we can only play the odds. Good parenting will increase the chances of children doing well. But it is only one factor. Children can only do as well as the cards life deals them. Their talents, temperament, health, and specific journeys through childhood will all play a part in how their lives turn out. Not just their parenting.

More than that, if we take the project manager approach to parenting and think that our efforts are the be-all and end-all of our children's success, we risk missing the real beauty of our children as unique individuals who grow and change in ways we can't predict or control. By trying to fix the result and out-maneuver the ever-present fear in being a parent, we risk missing the wonder. Parenting isn't a project you can complete. It's a story of lives lived alongside each other. Complex, messy, unfair lives in which difficult things happen and families have good and bad moments.

> **"To be a truly resilient parent, you need to stop blaming (yourself, your partner, your child) and settle for being good enough."**

Good enough means providing a fundamentally loving and supportive environment but not trying to meet our child's every need or being hyperattentive. Good enough means failing our children in ways they can handle so that they learn to become competent in navigating the world independently. It means accepting that not always being there for our children and letting them down (in small ways) enables them to grow and find their feet. Good enough involves getting it mostly right but sometimes getting it wrong. It means loving your children enough to let them get on with becoming who they will be and not regarding them as ours to shape or as badges of our success or bolsters to our self-esteem.

Our children's childhood isn't a journey we can control; we can only hope to influence it. If we think we can control it, we risk being knocked over or resorting to blame when life blindsides us with an unexpected challenge. Your child will experience hurts and disappointments, illnesses and falls. They may not go on to become anything like the young adult you have in your mind's eye. They will not make all the choices you wish for them. Their lives may be scarred by poor mental health, addiction, or economic hardship, and there is nothing you can do about it. Their hearts will be broken (and it will hurt). How they turn out is an as-yet-unwritten story, and yours is not the only hand on the pen.

Love your children, please, but don't overinvest. Don't be self-important and think that your input matters more than it does or take their outcomes to be a judgment on you. You need to look after yourself and be resilient (just as your children are) in order to keep going through whatever life holds in store. You have to get up again and again and keep trying to connect and enjoy the moments, no matter what happens or who your children turn out to be. I understand your children are the most precious people in the world to you and that you want to make everything alright for them. But you can't. Good enough parents know that we are all just making it up as we go along. And that's OK. Because that's the only way parenting can be done. Good enough parents learn to be comfortable with never knowing whether they have made the right decision or said the right thing. Good enough parents know they cannot control who their child becomes or what befalls them, but they can keep walking alongside them.

Because, ultimately, being a parent who loves and tries and recognizes when we get it wrong, who builds a relationship with our children based on love and true curiosity about who they are and who they will become, is being the absolute best parent anyone can be.

(And it's a lot more important than whether they remember their gym clothes.)

Further Resources

Anita Cleare, Positive Parenting Project: You will find lots more tips, discussions, videos, and ideas on my website at www.anitacleare.co.uk.

Babies: If you want to learn about infant psychology and how to tune in to your baby's signals, *The Psychology of Babies* by Lynne Murray (Constable & Robinson, 2014) is a helpful and practical read.

Child Development: For a quick and easy-to-read guide on child development across different ages, see the CDC's child development pages at www.cdc.gov/ncbddd/childdevelopment/.

Emotional Development: You'll find invaluable techniques for nurturing your child's emotional development in *The Book You Wish Your Parents Had Read* by Philippa Perry (Pamela Dorman Books, 2020).

Family Well-Being: The Action for Happiness website is full of simple practical ideas for the whole family for boosting resilience and well-being (www.actionforhappiness.org).

Healthy Living: Find advice from the American Academy of Pediatrics on all aspects of child health and well-being at www.healthychildren.org.

A Meaningful Life: For science-based insights on a wide range of topics relating to happiness and well-being, take a look at the online *Greater Good* magazine at www.greatergood.berkeley.edu.

Mindfulness: The Mindful website provides tips on meditation and guided meditations to help you practice at wwww.mindful.org.

Overparenting: To understand more about how overparenting undermines children's development, read *The Gift of Failure* by Jessica Lahey (Harper, 2016).

Parenting for Brain Development: *The Whole-Brain Child* by Daniel J. Siegel and Tina Payne Bryson (Bantam, 2012) is an unmissable read if you are interested in how to parent to nurture your child's brain.

Play: The internet is jam-packed with play ideas for children. But you can't beat your and your child's imagination as a source of play ideas!

Positive Parenting: For evidence-based advice on using positive parenting strategies, turn to Triple P® at www.triplep-parenting.net.

Positive Psychology: If you want to learn about positive psychology, the book *Authentic Happiness* by Martin Seligman (Atria Books, 2004) is a great place to start.

Positive Psychology in Education and Parenting: The Character Lab website is full of actionable insights from research that parents and educators can implement to support children's well-being (www.characterlab.org).

Index

About the Author

Anita Cleare, MA, AdvDip, is a parenting speaker, writer, and coach who supports working parents to balance successful careers with being a parent. Anita has an academic background in developmental psychology alongside extensive professional experience supporting families. She speaks at events for working parents across the United Kingdom and internationally and delivers parenting seminars and one-to-one support. Her advice is regularly featured in the media, including *The Sunday Times Magazine*, the BBC, and the *Telegraph*. Anita writes the award-nominated *Thinking Parenting* blog. To learn more, visit anitacleare.co.uk.